The Omitted Tribe Stories: Sheol Pt. 2

Brooks Crittenton

Royal Media and Publishing
Jeffersonville, IN
http://royamediaandpublishing.com
royalmediapublishing@gmail.com

Cover Design: Gad Elite Book Covers

ISBN-13: 978-1-955501-39-2

Printed in the United States of America

Reviews

From the moment I cracked this book open, I knew it was about to be a whole experience but I didn’t expect to be this locked in. If you know me, you know I love Greek mythology, so off top, this had me excited. But baby, the way TLK brought those mythological elements to life? Yeah… it’s giving elevated, it’s giving intentional, it’s giving “don’t talk to me, I’m reading.” Every page felt rich, layered, and lowkey divine. Let’s talk about the vibe because this is not just mythology. It’s mixed with that Shakespearean era drama… the kind that’s poetic but still hits. The tension, the language, the emotion, it's real deal storytelling. I’m not even gonna play with it: the author is coming for William Shakespeare’s throne. Like respectfully… move over sir.

Super proud of my friend. This isn’t just a read… it’s a whole vibe.

- Arabian Nites

The Omitted Tribe Stories: Sheol Pt. 2 is a vivid and emotionally charged continuation of a poetic fantasy world that blends mythology, darkness, and spiritual undertones into a unique storytelling experience. Written in a lyrical, almost spoken-word style, this book stands out not just as a narrative, but as an artistic expression. One of the most compelling aspects of the book is its poetic structure. Rather than relying on traditional prose, the author uses rhythm, repetition, and short-form verse to tell the story. This gives the narrative a raw, almost prophetic tone—like you're not just reading events, but feeling them unfold. Lines describing places like "Deathly Shadows" create a haunting atmosphere where survival feels fragile and fear is constant. That said, the book can feel intense and sometimes overwhelming. The fast shifts between characters, poetic format, and heavy symbolism may require readers to slow down and re-read certain sections to fully grasp what's happening. But for readers who enjoy immersive, thought-provoking storytelling, this becomes part of its charm rather than a drawback.

Overall, Sheol Pt. 2 is not just a story—it's an experience. It feels like a blend of epic fantasy and spoken-word poetry, driven by emotion, imagination, and a desire to leave a lasting imprint. The author's ambition to create something culturally impactful and comparable to legendary works is clear, and this book reflects that passion.

- Mark “Con9uctor” Freeman

Rating 5/5
A powerful, poetic journey through darkness, purpose, and transformation—best suited for readers who appreciate depth, symbolism, and creative storytelling.

ROYAL MEDIA
AND PUBLISHING LLC

Dedication

As always, I give all praise to The Most-High for protecting and giving me this gift to write

My wife for pushing me to chase greatness, I love you for that.

To my family, friends and fans chase any dreams you have and put God first.

ROYAL MEDIA
AND PUBLISHING LLC

Places

Judeawai is the beautiful city which has been practicing centuries worth of peace

Komodi Island is the training grounds for future queens sister's.

Characters of Sheol

Elijah	Poe's friend
Aiyden	Orion's friend, an accomplice of disrupting the Peace
Poe	Peace on Earth The chosen new king
Aminah	Poe's Girlfriend The chosen new queen, an angelic being
Mrs. Nia	Poe's Mother
Muna	The older twin to Luna
Luna	The younger twin sister to Muna, who is attuned to the moon
The Old Man	Crazy old man in Judeawai and for a long time he predicted destruction from the skies
Orion	A follower of the shadows
Rose	Aminah's enemy, who is committed to duty
Erykah	Aminah's Mother

Mother Kawana	Mother of the village, who watches all the children
The Mysterious Lady/ Lady in Shadows	Made such plans to disrupt the ceremony.
Queen Kathleen	Queen of Judeawai
Mycki	A protector and guide for a queen and future king.
Acai	Was thought to be dead
The Shadows	An elite organization disrupting centuries of Peace
King Jodi	The nature took his life.
The Master	The owner of Elijah
Azel	He was supposed to be the next heir, he is of royal blood, the son of a savage.
Ravana	A general in the making
Sheagle	Protector of kings
Axel	Father of Azel, a proud man with royal blood, his family was promised to be next in line
Lady Aponi	Wife of Karuk and tribal leader
Sir Mato	Tribal Leader
Sir Reme	Tribal Leader
Karuk	Husband of Lady Aponi and tribal leader
Nuka	Aponi's Brother
Sir Takoda	Father of Aminah

Mintz	Close to the family of Lady Aponi and Karuk
Andrea	Sister of Queen Kathleen
Ella	Sister of Queen Kathleen
Aphora	Sister of Queen Kathleen
King Denali	The last royal king of Judeawai before Jodi
Queen Kassi	The wife of King Denali
Tay	The big brother to Tey and man of strength
Tey	The younger brother to Tay and a man of wit
Erak	A man of myth
Lady Aveena	Mother of Lady Aponi and Nuka. Mother-in-law to Karuk. The leader of Komodi Island
Luther	Protector of Poe
Komodi	The demon from underneath

ROYAL MEDIA
AND PUBLISHING LLC

Table of Contents

ROYAL MEDIA
AND PUBLISHING LLC

Recap

A nightmare came true
Fire fell from the skies
Judeawai's king recently died
Who will lead these people?
A broken heart lifted an angel so high.
Poe is trying to survive the attacks from Azel and Ravana.
Aminah is alone after finding her best friend, Rose betrayed her.
By telling the tale to Luna and Muna, the twins
After such news she changed into a half angel.
Can this pain be healed?
Elijah is a slave, framed for something he didn't do.
Aiyden and Orion pointed to Elijah.
Mistakes were made at a party.
Some of the Tribal Society members desire royalty in the throne.
Can a future king write his wrongs?
In these destructive times.
An old man jumps with joy knowing he wasn't crazy.
The Shadows hide behind the scenes.
There's a secret lady controlling things.
Was king Jodi right about Poe?
Queen Kathleen is hurt, she lost her king Jodi
Mycki is now a guide for queen Kathleen and Poe
How will these characters move forward

In These Unforgiving Times
The world shook
Flames fell from the skies
So many ruined lives
Is it possible Poe can make things right
Who will be the new king and queen
In these unforgiving times

ROYAL MEDIA
AND PUBLISHING LLC

11. Folk Tales of Deathly Shadows

The rope was tightening around Elijah's wrist.
Why would Aiyden lie again?
Setting up the future king and himself,
Why would he do such a thing?
"Poe, the city will know your lies;
Purge in this fire!"

There was commotion outside.
Who was this voice calling from the skies?
"Poe! This is for your crimes!"
Elijah thought he heard Aminah cry.
At this time, a man was tugging harder on the rope tied to Elijah.
He needed to find a way to escape because Mrs. Nia was still alive.
Poe asked for Elijah's help,
A bigger reason to escape to help Mrs. Nia survive.

As Elijah looked at the skies to pray,
He saw the pure white clouds marbled with gray turn black
And blue skies turn scarlet red.
The sky opened and fire rained down on his village.
Balls of fire!
Someone just brought destruction to the city.

Elijah couldn't believe the Old Man was
telling no lie.

"Poe! This is because of your lies!"
Aminah was speaking about Poe's lies.
Elijah wondered how she found out.
The group was moving, trying to find cover
or protection.
Really? Whatever.
Elijah's wrists were hurting, burning.
He couldn't shake the image of Muna and
Luna laughing.
"Move faster, slave!" The man yelled.
Pouring from the skies were more flames.
Where was his homie in all this madness?
His main question was—

Why Did Aiyden Cause This
What made Aiyden so scared to tell a secret?
Why was he so bloody and barely moving?
Orion held him up and they both were
accusing him.
Now, I am a slave!
Is this mayhem a reason why people are not
being honest?
Poe admitted his mistake as he was passing
the chronic;
Talking about his obsession with women.
To me, I thought he was just living.
But these crimes are different.

Aiyden and Orion…I warned Poe they were the type to set him up.

Running faster, dodging fire, the squeals got higher and louder.
People were escaping.
Elijah saw someone being burned alive.
He was no longer thinking—just surviving.
The one holding the rope had his men with him.
There was fear in the eyes of some, and others just wanted to go home.
Their emotions have been shown.
Aiyden will pay for his wrongs.
Elijah's wrists were swollen from being pulled by someone so strong.

One of the men urged, "Let's just let the boy die."
The man holding the rope looked at his men
And cautioned, "He's worth more alive."
Elijah thought about the morning
He was getting ready for this celebration and was excited
Because he knew the two who were part of the ceremony.
Everything changed when Aiyden told him
Orion was linked to a mysterious lady.
That was bone-chilling and caused Aiyden to do something crazy.
Why wouldn't anybody believe him?

The taste of blood was fresh in Elijah’s mouth
He watched as fire ceased to fall from the skies.
A few members of the Royal Army were passing by
They stopped the man holding the rope.
Looking curious, they asked, “What are you doing with this boy?”
The one holding the rope replied, “He's charged with a murderous crime.
We are moving to the next town to find protection.
Let the King and Queen know he's doing hard labor in slavery.
His sentence will be life since a life was taken.
Not just a life, he took one of our women.
He will suffer for the rest of his life on Earth.”

After a long pause, a soldier hit Elijah in the stomach, saying,
“You're lucky we ain't got a hold of you.”
Coughing from all the smoke, another soldier chimed in,
“I would have beaten him within an inch of his life.
He wouldn't be walking.”

Screams from Judeawai grabbed everyone's attention, immediately snapping them back to the present.
The man holding the rope said, “We're heading towards—”

__Deathly Shadows__
A place you'll fear to go
The only option is survival
There, death is too easy
You'll dance on a thin line
A town forgotten
Rarely spoken of
Let the King and Queen know,
We're heading towards Deathly Shadows

Elijah couldn't believe what he just heard.
There was no time to process this as the man continued tugging.
Army men were running towards the city, ready to deliver the message.
How did everything change from him picking up the phone and hearing,
His homie say, “Hello,” to now be headed to the town, Deathly Shadows?

****

One of the soldiers looked at the other saying, “We got to tell the King of his crime; he's the reason for the fire from the skies."

"Did you hear where they were about to take him?" The other soldier responded

"Yeah, Deathly Shadows; I've heard stories of that town since I was a child."

"For real, I thought it was a myth, stories heard that children don't forget.

<u>The Tales Of Deathly Shadows</u>

Parents would say, if you become bad
The Shadows will swallow you
And you will become evil
Do not talk to the Shadows
It will bring hatred
The town is full of death
You smell it on the town's folk breath
Those were the tales of Deathly Shadows

As they looked ahead, and were shocked by what they saw.
An Old Man was skipping in the air
Laughing at everyone's despair
Yelling to the heavens
How sane he is.
As we passed him by, I noticed tears in his eyes
Not from sadness, but from happiness.

12. Damaged Flowers

There was smoke everywhere.
Vultures circled over her in the sky
Watching Aminah cry
Dead bodies were all they saw in their eyes.
She dreamed of fire falling from the skies.
In the distance, she heard the children cry
The ones who watched their parents die.
They tarnished her ceremony
And destroyed centuries of Judeawai's celebration.
Who was she looking at in her reflection?
On the left side, Aminah looked like a creature.
There was a weird resemblance to her great-grandmother
Even though they had never met, she knew it was her
Holding herself singing—

All I Wanted Was You
Why didn't you want me too?
All I knew was you
This used to hold so true
All I loved was you
Why didn't you know all I wanted was you?

A so-called friend of hers crossed a line
Then Rose ran through her mind
The only question she had was “Why?"

Touching the left side of her face
Marveling at the wing extending from her left shoulder
Where pieces of fabric lay on the intricately stitched dress
"How could he?"
Through the left eye, she saw a woman standing by the side, staring at her.
She was a woman of wisdom who embodied freedom.
Looking at Aminah, she smiled and said,
"You can finally see your guide; you've grown an incredible eye."
Aminah didn't have anything to say other than—

Why Was It?

Why was it I, who had to call destruction from the sky?
Why was it I, who had to deal with last night's lie?
Why was it I, who had a friend who pushed past unforgivable lines?
Why was it I, who was the one whose face became disfigured?
Why was it I, who caused the children to cry?
Why did I have a friend whom my future king wanted to try?
Why was it I, who was the only damaged flower?

"Why was it I?" Her guide inquired

__Do You Know Who I Am?__
I am you
I am I
I am the past and present
I am past mistakes
And future lessons
With that special eye, do you know who I am?

Aminah thought about her reply.
It was predicted that she would bring destruction from the skies
Last night she had a dream about it.
Aminah wondered if it was the way Poe touched her
His touch, she felt.
Forbidden love was made.
Her heart still melts.
How could he give Rose the same?
His look could release waterfalls—
Stains in drawers.
Just this morning, while brushing her hair
And looking in her grandmother's mirror
Realization set in.
Looking around frantically for her mother.
In all this destruction how could she possibly find her?

****

"How am I going to find my daughter?
I need to get to my baby.
I know she is lonely, she needs me,"
Erykah expressed to Mother Kawana
"Also, how was your son involved?" asked Erykah.
Mother Kawana answered, "My son is of royal blood. I overheard enough to know there are people ready to interrupt our government.
And I believe my son is caught up in it."
Erykah looked at Mother Kawana and asked, "Is this the cause of royal blood claiming the throne?"
Mother Kawana stared at the floor,
then looked at Erykah and replied,
"That's what I believe. We all witnessed destruction replace our peace."
Again, Erykah said, "I need to find my baby, she tried to tell me a dream,
No, a nightmare, and I made her feel like she was going crazy."
Mother Kawana asked, "A nightmare?"
"Yeah, maybe something like Nia had twenty-one years ago.
I'm just remembering she also told you."
Mother Kawana replied, "I will never forget how she looked when she woke from her sleep."

Poe was screaming, and she was looking worried.
Erykah started getting angry,
“That boy lied, I heard my daughter cry and saw tears in those lovely eyes.
Listen to me now, when it comes to him—

We Will Meet In Due Time

The truth I will find
Damaging such a flower,
There's nowhere he can hide
Fury builds in my inside
It will be my daughter and me
If it comes to it, he will die
There will be a conclusion
When we meet in due time

Mother Kawana said, “Maybe she will have the non-royal suffer.”
“First, she needs her mother,” Erykah replied.

****

Rose’s arm and face were in so much pain.
After this day, she wouldn't look at Aminah the same.
Someone who once called her a friend.
How could she forget how the flames chased
Some boundaries had been crossed
Beauty was taken away

She smelled her flesh.
Resting her head on Luna's lap,
Tears continued to flow.
Why did things get so crazy?
I wonder where the mysterious lady is, Rose thought,
Did she know these events would bring such destruction?
Her pain was intense
Shouting out, “My face!”
Then she started to think—

<u>These Thorns</u>
Will cause a prick
The type to make your blood drip
These thorns will stick
A Rose has been burned
The beauty will not survive
My defense will keep me alive
A special power has blessed me with these thorns

Rose listened as she heard Queen Kathleen cry.
There was a growing anger inside.
Knowing this wouldn't be something she could hide.
One of the Queen's ladies standing by was watching the girls
Noticing how Luna was consoling the girl with the burnt face.

She asked Muna, “Y'all sure you never met this girl?”
Muna answered, “We have never met her. We saw someone in pain, and my sister wanted to console her.”
“Mycki?" they all heard the Queen call out.
Rose’s mind started drifting about—

(Last Night)
She remembered sitting in that room, looking so good
Staring at her reflection
Body in shape, mask on the face
She had an opportunity to be anybody
Dripping with excitement, her lips she was biting
Everything about the party was a mystery
Dancing in front of the mirror, so petite
Oh, she knew no man could ever resist
The music playing in this dim room
She's all alone, deciding to pick up the phone
Dialing Aminiah's number, “Hello.”
“Girl, you coming out tonight?”
“I don't think I'll be able to make it, have fun though, I'll explain it tomorrow,
Call me in the morning,” said Aminah.
The phone clicked.
As the room grew darker, she knew who was in the room with her.
“Oh, look at this beauty. Peace will fall,

he can't resist this royal's body."
Rose, smiling, shifted the conversation,
"I called Aminiah, she's not coming."
The lady in the shadows commented,
"We're finally approaching the hour.
Rose, I need you to know that you're—"

<u>This Flower</u>

You're a treasure
A friend of beauty
Your thorns will bring mourning
You are someone to be noticed
Irresistible and clever
Between the both of you
I would say you're better
Polish those petals, walk your path
Blossom in this hour
He will pick and sniff and hold this flower

"Poe looks handsome in there, enjoying himself with no care. These dangerous actions towards a lotus, why would you dare?"
Rose looked at herself in the mirror and said, "I want him too; it's not fair."
"You know this would damage her."
"Well, you said, between the both of us,
I was better. Sometimes I wonder if she will give up her position with no effort.
In the art of secrecy, I learned from an expert; in this action, she will be hurt.

Never knowing it was her best friend."

The lady in the shadows said, "It's time to go get him. A bachelor deserves booty whenever."
Butterflies were floating in Rose's stomach now.
"You make me very proud.
You will be the lethal weapon by my side when I get the crown.
Go in there and grab him; let your love come down."
The lady in the shadows began laughing as she was leaving.
Rose could hear herself breathing.
Still buzzing from the drinking
No longer caring about anybody's feelings.
There's a different vibe when you see smoke under the ceiling,
Playing in dim light. This was her night, and she knew—

<u>He's Going to Bite</u>

The mood is feeling right.
This party has gone well into the night
I will grab his hands
Follow his every demand
Let him know he is The Man
This was the perfect plan
He's no king, he's weak
I'll show him tonight; he's going to bite

(Present Time)
Her thoughts got interrupted when she heard Queen Kathleen crying,
“Mycki, I know who brought destruction from those skies;
It was an Old Man. He predicted these times; I will never forget his face.”
That was the last thing Rose heard before she closed her eyes.

****

It killed him inside, that he had to give up the search for his daughter.
While trying to get through the woods,
he experienced a screaming sound,
Shaking of the ground, fire, and destruction from the skies.
Why was he witnessing these times?
Today was supposed to be a special day,
He was going to surprise her
Just to see her smiling in that dress.
The one his grandmother stitched up
All of a sudden, The Man saw something rising from the ground
It looked like the dead were sprouting out
The decay smelled of rotting flesh.
In front of his very eyes, he couldn't believe it.

In mere moments, the corpse looked like a living human.
Before The Man realized what he was doing,
His sword sliced through the neck.
The body fell, the skies were calling.

Following the light, the same one from that one night
A beautiful moment turned into a fight.
It was his choice to leave The Society.
The disruption of peace was the Royal's doing.
As he moved through the woods,
slicing more heads off the dead
He said, “I knew it, this type of destruction I couldn't be a part of.”
The only thing he stood on was—

<u>His Purpose</u>
To protect and guide her
Being a better husband
Loving on my woman
To teach survival in the wild
How to embrace the inner free
That light will shine bright
He will find strength in his purpose.

He could feel that he was getting closer
Blood was slowly dripping down his sword
His family would be the only thing he'd die for.

****

Aminah stared at her ripped dress,
“I remember when I stitched it,
Every thread, every piece of it, just for your great-grandfather.
The wedding he worked for it,
I wanted to work hard for something.
So excited I was to be next in line to sit in the seat of Royalty.
I needed to impress.
My mother taught me how to stitch.
So I will make a dress, and anyone who sees it will not forget.”

Aminah looked at the angelic being just sitting and smiling
“Why you? Isn't that what you asked?
You were born in jealousy.
You have a spirit.
You can't trust loved ones, friends, and family.
That little scream of yours opened a door in Sheol.
Those times when it was biblically deadly
Before the three generations of peace
Something you wouldn't want to see.
The wronging of ourselves was in our own genetics.”

Aminah sat there listening, trying to replay everything in her head.
She remembered making some good forbidden love.
Something she couldn't get enough of.
Getting dressed, the bathroom,
Hearing Rose's secret
Caused fire, cries, and villagers died
Everyone saw her.
She knew she had to hide.
Getting up.
Aminah looked at her, still smiling
The Being replied, —

<u>We're Waiting</u>

Be patient
We're waiting on your fleshly guide
This protector will help you survive
I know they're coming, so we're waiting

Her new wing swung and slapped her in the face.
Frustrated, Aminah asked, "Wait?"
The Being spoke, "Baby, what we are about to be dealing with next is tribulating times.
By any means necessary, we just have to try.
To be Queen, never forget you are next in line.
Now, your head, the village might ask for
I will make sure we're equipped for survival."

The Being stopped talking and looked behind Aminah
She swung around, now stuck in time.
The only words she could say were,
"You're alive!"
Her feet took her, she ran into his arms, and cried
Holding on to her tightly, saying—

"I Will Let You"
I will let you be innocent.
Baby girl, you can still be free
Your father will protect you
No one else will be able to harm you
I will let you be my daughter

13. A New Beginning

"Poe should be safe in that place.
I left him warm in the room."
Mycki speaking his thoughts out loud,
Everyone's running around.
How would he find the King and Queen now? Children were running,
Parents were chasing.
All Mycki could hear was 'The Dead are Living.'
Observing the area, he saw some of the Queen's ladies surrounding someone.
"Queen Kathleen," Mycki yelled.
Watching as one of the ladies started looking around
Running closer to them, he yelled once more, "Queen Kathleen!"
He saw her look up at him and asked, "Mycki?"
He ran towards Queen Kathleen
"Yes, it's me, my Queen. I need to know where the King is?"
Queen Kathleen started to cry, then she screamed—

"They Took Him Away"

"Mycki, they took our King away
His death will be remembered today
I prayed that he would be safe

A husband he was, a man he was, a King he is
It's hard to fix my lips to say
“They took him away.”

Queen Kathleen looked into Mycki’s eyes and stammered,
“The King is dead; he was burned alive.”
Everything the Queen said was registering in Mycki’s head.
That's why Ravana was trying to kill Poe.
Then Mycki urged, “Queen, we have to go.”
He told her of a law he just remembered,
“If the King dies of a natural disaster,
The King Announced will be protected for the duration of his time,
Unless one takes his life with their own hands.”
The Queen, quivering, responded,
“Mycki, I know who brought destruction from those skies;
It was the Old Man. He predicted these times. I will never forget—”

<u>His Face</u>
Was waiting for destruction
He seemed sinister in these times
It was the way he looked at me
The disgrace on his brows
There was so much hate in his face

As she was explaining the Old Man, a few soldiers were approaching.
Hearing their Queen's weary voice, they looked around, eyes searching.
Then one asked, "Where's the King?"
A faint voice revealed, "He died."
Queen Kathleen roared,
"The Old Man took his life!"
One of the army men disclosed,
"We passed one by,
He was yelling to the heavens, claiming to be sane
While laughing at everyone's despair
Skipping in the air
Tears of happiness."

The Queen commanded, "Get that Old Man who took my King from me!"
Three soldiers ran back in the direction from which they had seen the Old Man.
One of them confided to Mycki, "We saw someone with a young man.
He was tied to a rope heading towards Deathly Shadows."
Mycki's mind went racing, and he knew what his new priority was—

The King Announced

The one next in line
This King requires the right training
He will need it in these trying times

Leaving Poe alone
No protection in that home
Training hasn't begun yet
The King Announced, he must protect

Looking at the soldiers, Mycki questioned, "Deathly Shadows?"
"Yes," one of them replied, "They claimed it was for a murderous crime."
Mycki was trying to figure out what to do.
There was chaos going on everywhere.
He wondered, *Was it for the death of the King?*
He noticed three young women accompanying Queen Kathleen.
One was burnt on half her face, and the other two were twins.
At this point, everyone was looking at Mycki, so he had to think quickly.
"Queen Kathleen, we can continue this conversation, but we have to start moving.
I left the King Announced with no protection."
The queen's face was a blank stare.
She did not move.
"Queen Kathleen!" He thundered.
She looked into Mycki's eyes and realized they needed to leave now.
Luna tried to get up, nudging Rose to wake her, and gently said,
"Come on, Rose, it's time to wake up."

Rose opened her drowsy eyes and got up.
Muna was dusting herself off and walking in their direction to help them both up.
Never in a million years did Mycki dream
Today was the day he would see Sheol.
Now, he believes in the lessons they taught him about —

Sheol

A fiery place where the evil go
Hate, killing, and destruction are daily consumption
If you find yourself on that path
You will be almost there
Adir, the Almighty, always makes your path clear
But you have to listen through your ears
That place births fear
You will burn on this road
Beware of Sheol

Gathering together, they decided the chosen must be protected.
Moving together, Mycki looked at his Queen fighting grief.
There was a painful grimace on her face.
She was shocked that Jodi got taken away
This was supposed to be a special day.
Mycki knew he had to get them to the—

Safety Place

Generations ago, it was built for kings
If they were ever in need
Ducked low, it's said it's protected by prayers
If there's jeopardy, they provided security
The people built their king a Safety Place

Queen Kathleen fearfully asked Mycki,
"Is this real?"
Before Mycki could answer, they heard.
"Kathleen!"
Her voice made their bones chill
Yet to a few of them, the voice was familiar.

****

Azel and Ravana were running towards the door.
Ravana realized Poe was still on the floor.
Furious inside, he knew he should fight.
Glancing towards Azel, he said,
"We must not fail."
Ravana felt the heat from hell.
It was two of them versus one person by himself.
Turning around with his weapon,
He was ready to beat Poe even more.
Azel turned and ran behind him.

Ravana understood that they had to take out the next in line
While giving Poe more kicks to the ribs and yelling,
"Remember me, kid? Oh, grunting he is,"
Ravana yelled.
After Azel kicked him and shouted,
"Quick, give me your weapon so I can end his life."
Ravana started reaching, then something didn't feel right.
There was a shift in the atmosphere.
In Poe's head, he heard a voice so clear saying—

<u>I'm Here</u>

Hang on, just a little longer
If you survive this
I promise you will be stronger
I'm here for the protection of Peace
With me, you will be free
I've escaped death
Just to protect my Peace
Guard your mind, I'm here

The house was shaking.
Something was clawing at the door.
It was trying to get into the house.
"Azel, what the hell do you think that is?"
Azel muttered, "It's something big."

Ravana thought this might be his last chance to kill the kid.
Getting closer to Peace, weapon in hand,
He realized that if he killed Poe, he would be king.
Now Ravana's mind was racing on these things.
The crown on his head would make his mom proud.

The noise from the door was getting louder.
Whatever was at the entrance had all the intentions of getting in.
Both of them were afraid.
The door busted open, and what Ravana saw made him really nervous.

Myths he heard
And stories were told
Of a creature that used to protect all the king's generations ago.
They would fly in the air, strapped up for warfare
Such creatures were called—

Sheagles
Loyal as a dog
Fierce as an eagle
K9s in their beak
Razor sharp claws in those paws
They were loyal to the kings

Massive wingspans for soaring
unimaginable heights
Fur for warmth from the chilling nights
And for prowling during days of wintery
cold
These are the stories that were told
Tales remain audaciously bold
They were Sheagles

Azel asked Ravana if what they were
looking at was real.
The breath from the Sheagle, Ravana could
feel.
At this moment, both men knew not what to
do.
Nor had they even noticed the Sheagle had
moved.
Suddenly, Azel found himself flying across
the room.
The Sheagle looked at the floor and saw a
battered Poe
For a long moment, the creature froze.
Ravana ran towards Azel, helping him to his
feet.
Pulling Azel and telling him, "We've got to
go."
Both knew survival meant making it out the
door.
Exiting the threshold and finally outside,
Ravana and Azel began to run for their lives.

Listening behind, they heard the Sheagle advancing
Both knew who the creature was seeking.
They felt it chasing while hearing screeching, searing sounds
Letting them know it was ready for a fight.

****

Orion was staring at the mask on her face
While his eyes would glance at her shape.
A few men grabbed Aiyden, handling him with great care.
Looking at Orion, the lady wearing the mask told him to follow her.
Saying, "She's got to get her babies, or more like little sisters."
Orion always felt some type of way when he stood in her presence.

(The Night Before)
He talked to this lady in the shadows.
She was still mysterious, despite giving him love for the way he treated the twins.
Orion showed a new boldness to the royal blood.
In front of everyone, they watched him learn the inner secrets of the twins.
In the shadows—

She Encouraged Him

This lady told little Orion he was bold
There should be a party to throw
Suggesting a masquerade, women in masks
And Poe demanded a party,
Where his actions
Would affect tomorrow, she encouraged him

(Back in the Present)

"Come on, it's time to go get them."
Speaking to Orion in an urgent tone
Hiding in the shadows, she marveled at the destruction.
Orion asked, "Was this supposed to happen?"
She waited a moment before she gave a reply,
reflecting on all the townsfolk who died.
Looking him in the eyes, she said, "I'm not going to lie.
I didn't think the events would turn out this way, but the mission remains.
The crown must be taken away."
Orion listened to everything the lady had to say.
He knew what side he was on.
It was time for the royals to be on the throne.

As they walked a little further, Orion thought he saw the twins up ahead.

He said to the lady, “I think those are the twins with some people up the road.”
With a smile, she said, “Well, I guess that’s where we must go.”
As they got closer, she recognized the queen
She yelled at the top of her lungs,
“Kathleen!”

****

Twins, a girl with a burnt face, and the queen's ladies were leaving for a safe place.
Queen Kathleen had to ask Mycki,
“Is this real?”
Then she heard a voice that could make your bones shiver “Kathleen!”
That voice was familiar to her ears—

<u>Reminiscing Memories</u>

Came flowing in from her younger years.
She sees a little girl laughing and playing around
Kathleen promised she’ll watch over her forever
Fairyland stories, the little girl would dream
They would play Princesses and make believe.
In the end, one of them achieved Queen
Such a voice brought reminiscing memories.

“Kathleen, is that you?” asked the lady with a mask on her face.
She was wearing a black coat that covered her beautiful shape
Queen Kathleen thought this had to be a mistake.
“Kathleen, you don’t want to say hello?”
Laughing and standing next to a young man who looked around the same age as the girls.
“I’ve seen all that was conspired, and I saw how it went down.
As a royal woman, I have come for the crown.”
Queen Kathleen couldn’t believe what this mysterious lady just said.
“I also told you as a little girl I, too, wanted to be a queen.”
Shaking in disbelief, Mycki was standing beside her.
He said, “You will not talk to our Queen this way.”
The Queen screamed, “Acai, I thought you were dead.”
“So you do remember, I was just a little child. You were an outlet for me,
Kathleen, you used to listen when I needed to speak. But a vow was made.
I’ve lived in the shadows waiting for this moment.
Like I said before, I came for the crown.”

Furious and taking a fighting stance,
Mycki said, “You will have to go through me first.”
A mask covered half her face, yet her smile was visible.
“The King is dead; he died of a natural disaster.
As we speak, the future King is being slaughtered and his mother was murdered today.”
Seductively looking at Orion, she pointed at Mycki and said, “Kill that man.”
Then, looking at the twins, she said, “Luna and Muna hold the Queen down.”
Realization kicked in when Queen Kathleen looked at the twins.
Understanding they were with her.
Before anybody could move, they heard a malicious sound.

****

Laughing, trying to hold in his tears,
For years, the Old Man thought he was mad.
Devastated and cheerful,
His dream came true.
Now he questioned who would be the King in due time.
Poe's name was mentioned in the skies
It spoke of his lies
I heard an angel cry, on this very night

From the flames, he wondered which government survived.
Chains were heard behind
It was a few soldiers he passed by
Was the Royal Army looking for him?
What crime has he done?
They came smiling and stated,
"The Queen wants you for your wrongs."
Now looking serious, this Old Man replied,
"I haven't done anything, let me be on my way."
Soldiers surrounded the Old Man.
One angrily shouted, "She described your face; Deathly Shadows is where you're going!"
The winds started changing
The Old Man had his fist balled up, snapped back, "For what crime?"
They all answered in unison,
"For the tears in our Queen's eyes,
For the orchestration of these troubling times, for playing life with some strings,
This crime is for the death of our King!"

****

Mother Kawana watched Erykah leave to search for her fallen daughter.
Her son, she must look for now.
"What was the Tribal Society plotting?"
Mother Kawana pondered

She was a mother to all these children
Helping different families raise them
It didn't matter if they were royal or not—

She Raised A Lot

Smiles she has seen
There were children in need
Wiping sweat off faces from nightmarish-type dreams
She was 'love' for all those who didn't feel love
Never at home, always in houses
While her son alone, always waiting
There were others she was bathing
And more children, she was craving
After having her son, her womb closed up
Her dream never stopped because she raised a lot.

She believed her son needed her now
Or was it too late?
His sins might just be too great.
Looking all over the place
Still trying to be safe
She wondered,
Why did Erykah do Nia that way?
I mean she listened when Erykah explained, but she saw pain in her eyes.

Mother Kawana knew at some point she would come across her son.

Was she willing to forgive him for any and all wrongs?
There was a familiar voice she heard,
very familiar to her
Thinking to herself,
"I was just thinking about you..."
Her thoughts got interrupted when she heard a malicious sound from behind.
Then, watching as two men ran by, she saw fear in one man's eyes.
"Mother," a voice she swore she heard.

Suddenly, she felt something sharp grab her.
The force knocked her to the ground.
This creature's roar was a malicious sound.
The beak had razor-sharp K-9 teeth.
A bird, a dog, it appeared to be.
It was Mother Kawana
Who the thing began eating.
Growling, snapping, and clawing at her feet
One of those claws cut extremely deep.
Immediately, her blood came gushing out.
"Someone help me!" she cried with a shout.

The creature's intense stare looked for signs
Mother Kawana was growing weak.
Aggressive clawing, more blood from head to feet,
At this point, she could not speak.
Teeth were tearing into her skin.
An image of Nia played in her mind again.

Mother Kawana screaming,
dying with no help to be found
Barely realizing she was being eaten alive.
Looking around, she saw fear in everyone's eyes
Then she heard a helpless voice sobbing, trembling,
"That's my Mother!"
Her son bore through the crowd,
Running to his mother
As he forced his way closer,
A man grabbed him back
Teeth were sinking deeper, tearing, and slinging blood
Mother Kawana was weakening
Tormented by pain, desperately screaming, then silence.

Mycki, Queen Kathleen, and all her ladies watched
The horrid scene had nobody moving
Shocked by what they were witnessing.
The girls made their way to the mysterious lady
Luna and Muna were holding Rose.
Muna noticed Orion and two other men,
One holding the other
As he grieved, pointing to the lady being eaten alive.

“That’s my Mother! Let go, you have to let me try,” he begged,
He wept until his body was wilting from the sight.

Acai looked at her people and told them,
“It’s time to go.”
While everyone else focused on the death of a Royal Mother,
Acai and all her people disappeared in the shadows.

14. A King’s Healing

(Before The Celebration)
“Did I smell eggs, pancakes, and bacon?”
Elijah asked
“Yeah, my mom woke me up with that breakfast smell. I love that aroma.”
Poe nodded his head while passing the herb to him.
“Before this ceremony even begins,
You are going to have me too lifted,”
Elijah grinned from ear to ear.
Poe looked at Elijah as he inhaled the smoke
Blowing slowly into the air, Elijah questioned Poe—

What Type of King Will He Be?
The answer was just
For non-royals, this Celebration was for us
Truth, he said
Honor until he’s dead
Looking after his mother
There will be many women
And a queen by his side
For his people, he’s willing to die
He answered all the questions I asked

Because I asked him what type of king he would be
Passing the herb back and forth,
Poe looked at Elijah and shared,

"I just want my mom to be comfortable.
She looked worried when I came home from the party."
Elijah asked, "Worried?"
"She's been worried ever since my name came up as the next King Announced.
Something has been bothering her, and I don't know what it's about."
Eyes set in the skies when Elijah replied,
"This is your special day.
The sins from last night will be forgotten today. Go in there with a smile.
Don't forget, tonight you'll be loving Aminah.
I'll bet you'll knock the crown off her head."

Both began laughing and coughing;
Then coughing and laughing.
Elijah was trying to catch his breath when he squeezed out,
"We better do this more often."
"Yeah, I'm just worried about the training, they say for kings it's grueling.
I heard it's worth it in the end; some learning lessons through misery."

Elijah sat listening and watching the townsfolk walking around.
Children ran by, then asked,
"What startled you last night?"
Poe looked at his homie and answered,

“Like the Old Man said,
destruction from the skies.”
Elijah noted, “That Old Man was out of his mind, literally crazy.”
Poe smiled, “Maybe.”

Dancers were shaking, and the drums were beating.
As the last of the smoke was passed,
Elijah commented,
“Not to be weird, but this ceremony is beautiful.”
He heard Poe respond,
“Why all this for me?”
Elijah was enjoying the breeze on his face,
wondering what Poe was thinking,
He heard the event lady tell Poe it was time to go inside and get ready.
Turning to him, she said,
“Elijah, there’s something I need you to get.”
As she began walking off,
Poe looked at Elijah.
“Hey, bruh, check on my mom, I haven’t seen her come in yet.”

(Present Time)
“Elijah, help me!” he saw her hanging on the pole, bleeding.
“Elijah, help me!” his thoughts were interrupted when he heard,

"Get that fire started, I'm ready to eat."
The men around Elijah started moving;
Some prepared for the meal,
while a few went in for the kill.
The man who put the ropes on his wrist just stood still.
Watching as his demands were fulfilled.
Elijah couldn't believe how any of this could be real.
Thinking it was a bad dream, and he was still in his bed,
Ready to wake up and get fresh for this Celebration.
"What do you think he's going to do to the boy?"
Two of the men were talking when Elijah overheard them.
Deep down inside, he knew he had to escape,
Knowing he couldn't find himself living in Deathly Shadows.

There was no question he needed to go.
Everyone fell quiet when they heard the sound of chains up the road.
Elijah heard one of them say,
"Sir, I don't think we should have told those soldiers we had a slave. We have a few Royal Army soldiers coming this way."
The leader looked at that man and asked,
"How many?"

"There are like three soldiers and somebody with them. We can't tell who he is?"
He looked at the man and said,
"Make sure everything I said gets fulfilled."
Then he quietly waited until the soldiers approached,
The soldiers finally came to the leader
"We're glad you didn't go far.
We were told to deliver—

<u>A Queen's Request</u>

The Queen gave a description
Describing this Old Man for the death of the King
She wants him to be a part of this slavery thing
Suffering in Deathly Shadows
After everything gets settled
She will certainly follow
Promising a reward for a Queen's request

The leader looked down at the Old Man
Then said, "This Old Man will not be able to handle my demands."
The army man who told Elijah that *he's lucky they didn't get a hold of him*
Looked at Elijah, then the Old Man, and said, "I don't care if on the walk they die.
The Queen wants this Old Man to suffer for his murderous crimes."

After handing the Old Man over to the leader,
The army men started to head back in the direction of Judeawai.
Then Elijah heard his Master say while walking away and smiling,
“Slave! Listen well, you two are now connected.
I don’t expect much from this Old Man, but if you decide to get out of line.
Your punishment will be that this Old Man will receive your strikes.
Remember now you are in control of his life.”

****

Screaming, holding onto Mycki, everyone jumped.
When they saw a dog/bird pounce on Mother Kawana.
The creature was chasing Azel and Ravana.
The way the creature was tearing and eating Mother Kawana had Ravana screaming
And trying to get to such a creature and kill it.
Azel was holding him back.
Mother Kawana started yelling,
“Someone help me!”
This scene had everyone's attention.
Its teeth were sinking into her skin.

Clawing at her body, blood was gushing.
“That's my mother!”
There was more biting and clawing—more blood was gushing.
We all heard Kawana crying; my eyes were glued to a…
Mycki yelled, “It’s a Sheagle.”
This monster was eating Mother Kawana alive.
Killing someone I've known my whole life.
“That's my Mother!”

She was the mother of the village,
An extra hand for helping raise these children;
Now, blood was everywhere—such a horrid scene.
I couldn't believe how much blood dripped from its beak.
As I pondered to myself, *how could this be?*
After it finished, the creature looked at me.
What made this monster notice a queen?
Then it started to scan the scenery,
looking for the two it was chasing.
Mycki realized it came from Poe’s direction.
This creature was angry, in every direction it was searching.

After all the commotion,
Queen Kathleen noticed the girls left with Acai.

A fire started to burn inside as she thought
of the girls she had helped survive.
Realizing they were a part of a plan that
caused her husband to die.
Queen Kathleen's attention was back on
Mycki when she asked,
"Did you say a Sheagle? What on earth is a
Sheagle?"
Mycki answered by saying,
"I heard about them in the myths.
They were protection for the king's back in
the times before peace."

The Sheagle's eye contact was back on
Queen Kathleen.
Moving closer to the Queen, she could feel
the vibration
When its paw touched the ground.
Mycki took a defensive stance.
At him, the creature glanced.
Stopping in front of Queen Kathleen,
it bowed, giving the utmost respect to her.
She returned the bow towards the creature.
Then it turned around and walked back in
the direction from which it came,
Yet looking back, as if it wanted them to
follow.
Mycki said, "Queen, I believe the Sheagle
wants us to follow it."
The Queen, her ladies, and Mycki followed
the Sheagle to the Safety Place.

As they got closer, they saw the broken door.
Stepping in, they saw the claw marks on the floor.
This was a place that no longer felt cozy.
Everyone stopped abruptly when they saw
Poe on the floor, holding a metal pole.
The Queen saw Jodi, and they all asked—

“What Have They Done To Him?”
Lifeless, he lay on the floor.
Cracked ribs for sure
An attempt was made for a life to be taken
All because he was chosen
His mother was murdered
In him, many saw that things were broken
Regarding our future King, what have they done to him?

Queen Kathleen told her ladies to grab the King
She must prepare for his healing….

****

Ravana bellowed, “It's your fault my mother died!”
“Ravana, please come here.”
“With your plan, you lied. The seat is not ours, and we tried.”
Acai looked at Ravana as he cried

"The plan will still get fulfilled."
Ravana blurted "My mother was not supposed to be included in those plans.
I tried to accomplish your every demand.
Why did it have to be my mother?"

Acai, trying to calm Ravana down, asked,
"What happened?"
Looking at her, he screamed,
"What happened?
What do you mean, 'what happened'?
Your plan failed!"
She replied, "Between you and Azel.
What happened?"
Ravana looked at her and said, "After our conversation, I connected with Azel.
He explained his plan, and we went our separate ways
Before the fire started raining.
I came across Poe, then beat him to a pulp.
I was really close to taking his life when
Mycki sucker punched me,
Then took the boy away."

She listened as Ravana broke down the events.
"I met back up with Azel, and he had news to tell. He informed me that Jodi No Name fell into the hands of a natural disaster.
Deciding the boy was who we must go after,
I knew Mycki's direction.

We found Poe in this Safety Place, and then we started beating him in the face.
Out of nowhere, I get hit with a lightning strike.
Azel challenged Poe—

Then He Failed

"Dropping the ball to someone inexperienced
He had a chance with Jodi, then lost to Poe
From my misstep with Mycki
Nature took away Jodi
Poe's life was going to be taken
Azel was coming close
There was a quick chance, then he failed."

"I hit Poe across the face and started to run away. As we ran, I felt a surge of anger.
There was a thought I wanted to beat more into his face
Running back, more kicks he got.
Before we could do anything too devastating, we heard something that'll make your heart stop.
We saw a protector of kings.
It was trying to take our lives.
We ran, and it followed us.
I saw that creature take my mother's life."
She looked at Ravana, grabbed his face, looked into his eyes, and declared,

"I will still become Queen and promise to
make this wrong right."

****

(Later That Night)

She cried out, "You were supposed to save
me, Elijah!
Why do you just sit there? Help me!"
Waking up, Elijah saw the fire was still
going and everyone was sleeping
After a night like this, he wondered what
everyone was dreaming.
His wrist was anguishing from the rope still
tied.
Moment by moment, wishing he had died.
Tears lingered in his eyes remembering Mrs.
Nia hanging lifeless.

The guard was sleeping—their leader was
resting
Nobody knew Elijah was up.
This was his last chance at escaping
Elijah started to crawl, quietly sneaking and
moving
Trying to watch his every movement.
The Old Man was oblivious to what the
young man was doing.
A sleeping guard was unaware
To take advantage of a night so rare.
Getting closer to the guard sleeping

Around his neck, the rope was creeping.
As he was squeezing, the guard was barely breathing,
Air was the one thing he needed.

Light wrestling, trying not to wake anyone resting,
Elijah held on while the guard's neck was breaking.
More squeezing, slightly moving,
Getting out alive is what he was relentlessly doing.
Elijah felt the life of the guard leaving.
More squeezing than moving,
With the intention of the guard's neck being broken.
So much strength and hatred,
This guard's life, Elijah would be taking,
And soon, he would feel his neck breaking.
Suddenly, Elijah felt the snap.
He stood behind the lifeless guard.
Tears were pouring,
Not knowing how to react.
He moved his arms from around his neck,
The guard fell to the ground.
Elijah's strength killed a man.

Around the dark camp, everyone was still resting.
A shimmer, he thought, could be a light.

Unexpectantly, Elijah felt a blow to his stomach.
Someone had swung with all their might,
For a second, he lost his sight,
Then heard—

<u>"I Will Beat You Within an Inch of Your Life"</u>

From one of my men, a life was taken
An opportunity was made
Take this hit to your face
Moving with speed, Elijah couldn't see
A man's life has been taken
Consequences that you will live out
Elijah felt multiple strikes
Then the slave Master walked over to the Old Man
Woke him up in the middle of the night,
Looked into his eyes and screamed,
"I will beat you within an inch of your life."

Holding on to the Old Man, he shouted, "Look, slave!"
Elijah tried to look at him, then one of the men
Lifted Elijah by the chin to make sure he was watching him.
The Old Man stood firm in front of the slave
Master, boss, leader, whatever.
He struck the Old Man to the ground with kicks and hits.

After a while, you could hear the sounds of breaking bones and ribs.
Elijah thought, *"How will this Old Man live?"*
Then came more strikes throughout the night.

Then the leader said to Elijah, "Slave! I have told you once,
I don't care about this Old Man's life.
You are now responsible for this.
Your punishment—the Old Man will receive your strikes."
Still smiling as the Old Man lay on the ground, the leader
Looked at both of them and said,
"Let me introduce myself as—"

<u>Your Master</u>
Y'all will address me as Master.
The controller of y'all lives
The only reason you're alive
Deciding to take one of mines
You will lend me yours
After this night, you will only call me your Master

****

Queen Kathleen watched as he lay there so still.

Oh, how they tried to kill her king.
On the bed, all she saw was Jodi,
The only man to have touched her.
She was his Queen.
Knowing he needed healing
Only she can give it,
Wiping her eyes, she slowly started
preparing
All she could see was Jodi.
He still had energy.
A chance at living.
More touching and breathing
Rubbing the blood throughout his body
She was going to save her Jodi.
Knowing she can't run this throne alone,
He would be there in the morning,
She needed her king.

His eyes opened and he asked,
"My Queen?"
Placing her fingers over his lips, she said,
"Shhh, my king, you need healing."
Stroking her hair with his hands,
Enjoying the silkiness of all her strands,
Jodi smiled at Queen Kathleen.
He asked her, "Can you heal me?"
She responded softly, "Of course, my King."
Then she started his—

<u>King's Healing</u>

Her hands rub over his body

Putting ointment over her Jodi
Whispering, she will always love him
Jodi was looking
Queen Kathleen was praying
His face was fading
The Queen was giving all her energy
But Jodi was leaving
Then Poe started appearing
The Queen began screaming,
Realizing she had given Poe a King's
healing.

15. Deathly Challenge

Azel couldn't believe he'd seen such a beast
With razor-sharp teeth between its beaks.
Both of them, it was ready to eat.
Protecting the newly King Announced
Huffing and puffing, still trying to breathe
Looking around, where could Ravana be?
Playing the events in his head
Fire from the skies,
Seeing the dead,
Not from his own hands, yet the King still died,
Even though he definitely tried.
A natural disaster caused the King's death
Finally, it was sinking in how—

He Lost Another Challenge
To a child with no heir
A king from the grave protected him,
It was not fair.
A mythical creature came out of nowhere.
Even with Ravana's help
Royal members were running and hiding
Reflecting on how he lost another challenge

Everything that happened today can't be real, Azel thought
"Someone opened a door to Sheol."
Heads sprouting up from the ground.

Even in this time, he'll be grateful to take the crown
He just needed to know how the plan failed.
Today was the day he felt hell's flame.
Then he remembered she had removed the shell from her face.
Deciding he must find them, he has questions,
And answers will be given.

****

A few tribal members were sitting in the council room
Trying to find protection from this fiery destruction.
One of the members inquired if anyone knew if the King was okay
Or if they saw any of the other members.
Just this morning, they were planning the Celebration of Peace.
"A few hundred years, it was supposed to be,"
One of them replied, "We haven't seen the King or Queen."
Another asked, "What must we do; how can we properly move?"
Acai's presence could change the whole mood.
They never saw her come into the room,

Yet, there was a certain darkness that started to loom.

Acai repeated the question,
"What should y'all do?"
The few members looked into her eyes.
All were surprised as they said, "You are…"
She finished by saying, "Let me introduce myself as—"

<u>Queen Acai</u>
She was beautiful and foolish.
Coming out of a womb to parents who didn't love her
Not knowing why
The shadows promised she'd be queen
But, her family, she had to leave
Now Queen Acai was cursed from head to feet
A chill runs up your spine when you see Queen Acai

One of the members alleged,
"You're no queen!
We only recognize Queen Kathleen."
Smiling as she strolled over to the royal member.
In front of everybody, with weapon in hand,
She plunged her sword through his spleen.
His wife, who was next to him, screamed from sheer shock.

Standing by her side, they saw Ravana, the second to Azel,
Giving the side eye to the man she stabbed,
Queen Acai said, in a snarky tone,
"Enjoy your sleep."

Around this new Queen were twins, a young man, and a girl with a burnt face.
One of the members said,
"They didn't understand."
So Queen Acai explained,
"Your King died of a natural disaster
I challenged your Queen Kathleen…but she didn't want to challenge me.
By law, I claim the seat to be Queen."
The wife of the husband who was just stabbed mumbled,
"So who will be your King?"
Queen Acai curiously looked at Ravana as if he were her answer.

****

Azel thought to himself,
I will be King since King Jodi is dead.
This matter must be brought before the Tribal Society.
Immediately running down the hallways, he proclaimed—

They Will See

Tonight, the Tribal Society will see
When a crown is on my head,
And I stand before them as their King
These lands will be led right
Tonight is the night they will see
I'll sit before them as King
All night I will be getting pleased by my
Queen
Oh my dear Tribal Society
We will only welcome the Royal Family
That day has come this night—they will see

There were dark shadows everywhere.
Down the hallway, a lady's voice he could
hear
Another voice he heard asked,
"What about Azel?"
He heard the woman answer,
"Ravana has told me the details and
Azel has failed another challenge.
We need a champion as king."

Azel couldn't believe what he was hearing.
Acai continued speaking
Thinking to himself,
Ravana was his second!
All this planning, never once did he claim
the throne
What vexes him to want the crown now?

He heard her voice in the room, and Acai said, "The throne will be open for those chosen to rule, until training for the King Announced is complete. For right now Poe and Aminah are still alive.
So, they have seven years to claim this seat.
If not, I will rule my term all the way out."

Azel thought of the times they fought together
Planning how they would make the Tribal Society better.
I told Ravana, "Once I become King,
the crown will go to 'me,' and I will share with him.
Ravana told me I was born for this.—"

<u>Why Would He Betray Me</u>
My second. What finally enticed him to want to be first?
Was it when the plans became worse?
We have been close since our training days.
Laughing at Jodi No Name
Did he want Queen Kathleen?
I need to know, 'Why would he betray me?'

Everything was cool when we were planning.
Something changed in him since he saw fire raining.

"The few leaders here can crown their new King and Queen," Acai said.
Azel stormed into the room,
"Glad you made it to the party, Azel,
Now, on your behalf, explain to these Tribal leaders how you failed."
He looked into the eyes of three Tribal leaders who were scared.
Ravana was standing by Acai.
"I thought you died."
She replied, "At one point, I did give my life."
Acai stared at Azel, the one who failed, then asked, "Would you like me to be your wife?"
Ravana was surprised by such a question.
"Whoever will be my husband will be king, for seven years, unless Poe comes and tries to claim the seat."
Azel thought, "King? It can finally be.
I can bring honor to my family."
"Of course I want to be King,"
Azel confirmed. "That's why I was going to take the King's life with my own hands."
"Yet you had a chance and then you failed again," she replied
"Well, Ravana failed his challenge because Poe didn't die." Azel said
With a big, grimacing smile on her face, she said, "Precisely.

Both of you have said each has failed, so I present—

A Deathly Challenge

Between the two, y'all will fight to the death.
One of you will have no breath
Now, both of you step up
Choosing a weapon, both had one in hand
The Second wants to be first.
A promised heir has one last chance to be king.
Out of nowhere, "Is that my father coming to watch me?"
Azel's astonished thought ranted on,
"How on earth could this be?"
After all these years, he couldn't show himself to still be weak.
Ravana said, "Azel."
Azel cut him off abruptly, "Don't speak!"
At Ravana, he leaped, striking at someone he once called *a friend*
Sweeping under his leg, striking,
trying to see him dead.
Azel's father was watching.
At the door of Ravana's life,
Azel was knocking
A solid hit to Ravana's jaw,
he fell on the floor.
Azel jumped on him for sure
But with his wrist,

Ravana blocked Azel's knife.
Azel kicked Ravana in the wound he got from the lightning strike.
Knowing this was the fight of his life.
Acai was watching Ravana fail.
Azel heard Axel, his father, say,
“Send him to hell.”
Lying on the floor, Ravana appeared as if he couldn’t take any more pain
Azel believed this was his only way,
for tonight, the crown would be placed on his head with a Queen by his side.
He watched as his father smiled, something Axel never did.
But before Azel’s final strike was thrown,
Mother Kawana flashed before Ravana’s eyes.
He remembered seeing a flesh-eating creature destroy her,
which gave him extra strength to see Azel as the creature.
The more he swung, the more blood Ravana would see,
Now he was slashing away and making Azel bleed.
Soon, Azel’s father’s excitement was disappearing,
The only thing Azel heard was,
“You disgust me.”
Ravana gave Azel more punishment than he had given him.

Azel thought to himself,
What was Ravana's motivation?
What did he see to cause tears on his cheeks?
The more horrid pictures of his mother, Ravana would see
He was determined to strike the bird, making sure it was hurt
Giving the final powerful blows to put Azel in the dirt
Ravana knew he survived a deathly challenge.

The leaders watched as their last hope failed.
"I need the signatures of you three.
You are the ones who will sign this decree.
Now crown your new King and Queen," demanded Acai
Ravana stood over Azel, watching him die.
Pondering how this dreadful day's end led him to take a comrade's life.
Ravana looked into the eyes of his new wife.
Confident that making this decision felt right
"Leaders, please sign," Acai told them.
Lady Aponi, Sir Mato, and Sir Reme all signed the document. "In these times,
Few can uphold a union. Thank you for your understanding," said Acai
As she immediately gave a direct order,
"Rose, come on, let's get you cleaned up.

Twins and Orion, please take their lives."
Pointing to the leaders who just signed,
"After it's done, follow behind, it's a
celebration! Time to enjoy our Ceremony.
Tomorrow we will inform the city of—

<u>The New King and Queen</u>
Of these troubling times
The city will chant or die
No more King Jodi and Queen Kathleen
From the shadows they rise
Both are now recognized
Respectively, The New King and Queen

Azel heard partying throughout the night.
Still, he was trying to fight for his life
Gasping for air—with none to spare
No one around, it was lonely in there
Dying on the floor was a royal heir.
Then he saw the man lying there
The reason all those leaders were scared.
Karuk, the husband of Aponi,
lay on the floor in a pool of blood,
Gushing from his body like a raging flood.
When everything was going on, why didn't
he see?
In his rash decision, some of the royal
members—

<u>They Did See</u>
Him be so weak

Falling at Ravana's feet
Once upon a time, they all believed in him
The crown didn't go to me
An heir promised to be king
Royal blood ran through his veins
Today, he felt the worst pain
When he failed
There was no pleasure from a queen
He disgraced his family; they did see

Final words for his father, who left without a care
"Why did the crown not go to me,
a promised heir?"

16. Just A Dream

"Are you going to love me forever?"
Aminah laid on Poe's chest, staring into his eyes.
After handing him a blunt, Elijah asked,
"If times got tough, would he even try?"
Aminah stood up, wearing a torn-up dress, looked at him,
And said, "I would have said yes."
He blinked, and again, on top of him, she was resting.
"Poe!" He heard his mother calling.
All over his body, Aminah's hands were moving,
"Are you going to pass that blunt?"
He heard Elijah ask
"Poe!"

No longer could Poe hear any background noises.
Aminah and him were together, like one with each other.
She started crying as they were kissing.
Through his window, he could see raining fire.
There was no couple's romance.
Just kids frantically running for shelter.
Death playing violin strings, taking lives.
Aminah was holding me with all her might, singing to herself—

It Was Going To Be You

My first love
My first fight
My first real reason to live life
My first union
It was warned
My first real hurt, it was going to be you

There was blood in her tears.
Aminah started floating in the skies.
The most beautiful woman,
his promised wife.
Pointing down, telling all the townsfolk
The scream was so clear
“This is because of your lies.”
He was beaten within an inch of his life.
Controlling lightning strikes.
Forbidden love was made,
She was looking at her torn dress.
He left a secret in the masquerade
(Everything begins to fade).
All he could see was his mother's face
In the kitchen, making breakfast
Cooking eggs and bacon.
Out of this hellish dream, Poe was awakened
Sweating and shaking throughout his body,
Pain was racing.
Why was he aching?
Towards his room, Poe heard footsteps
coming.

Standing to his feet
His room seemed different.
The smell in the atmosphere was unfamiliar.
Why were people not busy getting ready for the celebration?
There was no music, no instruments banging, the townsfolk were not singing.
Were his actions from last night the cause of no celebration?
Was he no longer chosen?
Coming to notice, he had scuffed his Chucks.
His door swung open, then he saw—

<u>His Queen</u>

She didn't look the same.
Queen Kathleen was different in a way
There was no light
No joyful glee in those eyes
Where was her fight?
It wasn't the clothes that looked plain
You could see it in her face
Something changed; a part of her has died
Permanent stains were on her cheek from when she cried
This was a new image of his Queen

The man who followed behind,
He'd seen him in his dream saving his life.
That man looked upon him and said,
"Poe, I am grateful you survived."

His whole body started aching again.
Bones were cracked within.
Poe thought to himself, *Who tried to take my life?*
The man kept speaking, then said—

<u>Our King Has Died</u>

The one we have honored is no longer alive
His life was claimed by the fire in the skies
There was a plot to take his crown, and some leaders tried
It was nature that changed the course of these times
When it happened, you could hear the painful cries
Judeawai was saddened when all realized our King had died

When he said such things, Poe remembered
He had seen King Jodi right before his eyes
Giving him the strength to wield a lightning strike.
Poe looked at the floor and saw the pole
Thinking out loud, Poe said, *I controlled lightning.*
Interrupting what Mycki was saying, all noticed Poe
Looking at the metal pole on the floor.
Mycki said, "When we found you, your hand had a death grip on that thing."

Poe replied, “It was given to me by the King.”
Queen Kathleen stared at the beaten young man who could barely stand.
Poe said, “He helped me produce a lightning strike, protecting me from the men who tried to take my life.”
Poe felt dizzy from standing up too long and started to fall over,
Mycki caught him and held Poe up by his shoulders.
He placed him in the bed and fluffed his pillow to relax his head.
Mycki was gabbing fast
Thinking to himself, *So this wasn’t a dream?*
Poe couldn’t pick up on everything
Mycki continued talking
Again he thought to himself, *Did he just say we have a new king and queen?*

The breakfast cooking in the kitchen made Poe's stomach start hurting.
Others who were around could see it in his face,
The Queen ordered one of her ladies to fix Poe a plate.
Refusing the help, Poe slowly got up and said,
“It's okay, I'll make my way to the kitchen.

That way, I can see what my mother's fixing."
The air drew its breath back.
At that moment, everyone was silent.
Mycki looked at Queen Kathleen,
She knew she had to say something.
Poe noticed how they looked at each other before asking—

<u>Where Is My Mother?</u>

The one who fights my fears and wipes my tears
The one who was there when I had nightmares
Your reaction shows that she's not downstairs
Where's my mother?
Elijah was supposed to find her.
She's an example of what it looks like to beat all odds
The fire couldn't have gotten her
She's an angel sent from the heavens by the One above
Strong, brilliant, and smart; her actions were led by her heart
She taught me love
I'm the future king!
Send out a search party.
I need to know WHERE IS MY MOTHER!
With tears in her eyes, the Queen replied—

She Is Not Alive

In the midst of the chaos,
Someone took her life.
The murderer was sentenced to Deathly Shadows.
A lady in the Shadows is our new queen
Someone brought this information to light
The one who birthed our future king, she is not alive

Time stopped
He thought *someone took her life.*
Deathly Shadows for his crimes?
Mycki and Queen Kathleen witnessed.
The maids looked in awe when they saw
Poe banging his head on the wall.

Blood he smelt
Queen Kathleen knew how he felt.
Grabbing the young man in her arms,
she held him.
He was weak in her embrace.
Poe cried, "Wake me from this dream."
They knew he would need strength to move in this new reality.
Anger in his eyes, Poe's tears were falling.
His grip tightened, asking the heavens,
"Why! Why?"
Breakfast in the kitchen no longer smelled good.

They all left him to rest in his room
Mycki looked worried.
When they were downstairs,
Queen Kathleen asked Mycki,
“What's wrong?”
Tapping his foot on the floor, he answered with her question—

<u>What's Wrong</u>

Our King has died
We now run for our lives
Everything about this situation isn't right
The boy upstairs barely survived
We're risking so many lives while we hide
Judeawai will never be the same
After Ravana and Acai
Tapping his foot, saying this is what’s wrong

She listened to his words.
Understanding every concern, then said,
“That young man, our future king, is hurt.”
Mycki listened nervously, looking around the kitchen.
“We have to leave tonight,” he expressed with concern.
Queen Kathleen stared Mycki in the eyes
Then she shrugged and replied, “Alright.”

Poe was crying and shouting,
“Who would dare take her from me!”

His tears were steadily streaming down his cheek.
From his window, in the distance, he could see the beach.
Those screams, his cry, were deep inside.
Queen Kathleen knew how he was feeling and felt guilty for his pain.
Him being alive was because of her healing.
As she was pondering these thoughts, the back door opened.
“She killed my sister. Mintz told me this and ordered the young ones to kill the elders.
I was out at sea when this happened.”
Said—

Nuka
Brother of Lady Aponi
Brother-in-law to Karuk
Vowing that he was going to kill this newly crowned Queen
For which she had taken
The oldest brother
Last of his bloodline—Nuka

While looking out the front window,
One of the Queen's ladies whispered,
“They're here.”
Nobody heeded her warning.
The man mourning his sister was seething.
Now the Queen’s maid screamed,
“They're here!”

Right before an arrow came through the window
Hitting the young maid.

Seconds later, Mycki heard the Sheagle squealing,
Nuka grabbed his weapon.
"Mintz take them to the ship."
Everyone was looking around.
Queen Kathleen ran to the maid.
All heard soldiers approaching the front door.
Nuka was ready to go before this fake queen.
He heard the agony of the young maid, who was dying.
Mintz yelled, "Let's go!"
Mycki grabbed Queen Kathleen towards the stairs,
The other two maids followed.
All of them started running, and then the front door burst open.
Nuka began running towards the fake queen.
But he found a sword through his spleen.
Nuka, the oldest brother, last of his bloodline, fell to the floor.
Everyone heard Queen Acai yell,
"Tell Aponi and Karuk I said hello!"

****

Poe was staring at the beach from his
window.
Waves crashed as the tide rolled, changing
sand to mud.
With thoughts of his mother,
whom he really loved,
Poe started curling on the floor.
The room started changing.
Pictures of his mother, he could see
Poe's will to live was getting weak.
This was his day, chosen to be king.
He bellowed,
"Who would dare take her from me!"
He was hurting—didn't see her forming.
Commotion he heard before hearing her
words—

<u>What's Wrong Baby</u>

At this moment, Poe knew he was going
crazy
Who was this smiling lady sitting on the bed
His tears she was wiping
Finding himself stuttering
Trying to say
"I…I… I thought you died"
Poe was her little boy when he cried
"Even when I'm gone, I'm here with you,"
she whispered
"I wanted to be there"
An animal squeal he heard in his ears
"Now, in a strong voice, say your name;

It's what I like to hear."
Poe replied in a firm voice,
"Peace on Earth, your little Poe!"
His mother started fading away,
While asking her son the question
'What's wrong, baby?'

There was movement coming up the stairs.
"Tell Aponi and Karuk I said hello!"
His door swung open
With fear in their eyes, Queen Kathleen
said, "We've got to go."

"Acai!" They all heard the skies cry.

17. The Mourning After

Destruction was seen in Judeawai,
Homes were devastated.
Family members were confiscated by death.
You could smell the dead in its breath.
How was it possible that fire fell from the skies?
This morning, you could hear the city cry.
An angel fell—then rose hell.

Sheol, a story you wouldn't believe.
It happened before our eyes.
A king died before his time.
As a people, the townsfolk were holding each other,
Praying for better.
Who has changed the weather from peace to distress?
What have we done to deserve such things?
Yesterday was supposed to be a celebration.
Generations rejoiced in stillness;
Communion, fellowship, and conversation
All those years wasted.

The dead have risen, breathing amongst the living.
Where's our Queen?
Who will lead in this time of need?

In the distance, ceremonious bells were sonorous.
"What is the reason for this ringing?"
The townsfolk were thinking after this devastation,
Nobody was prepared for what they were about to see.
Twins, a young man, and a few soldiers were following behind
They yelled, "Judeawai, our hope is in—

King Ravana and Queen Acai
Your Queen Kathleen is not here.
A natural disaster took our poor King Jodi's life
Honor our new king and queen
An elderly lady looked at the skies
Pleading for this to be a dream
On repeat, they heard
King Ravana and Queen Acai
What they're saying has to be a lie
Judeawai's heart would not accept King Ravana and Queen Acai

"Muna, come here!" Yelled Queen Acai, whose presence was chilling.
Muna walked to where the Queen was slowly, next to her King.
"Yes, my Queen," said Muna.
Queen Acai began a series of probing questions,

"Did what I asked get handled?"
"Yes, my Queen, those lives were taken,
And their bodies were handled," replied Muna.
"How?"
"My sister, Orion, and I took each life.
I saw their souls leave their eyes.
We each grabbed a body and dragged it outside.
Not too far away to a place all can see.
As they burned, the wind played with the smoke."

Intrigued, the Queen probed further,
"Why did you burn the bodies?"
Smiling Muna explained,
"Well, my first thought was
The people would believe they died in the fire."
Queen Acai, dwelling in thought, said,
"The decree was signed after the fire."
"At that point, then you're testing the crown," Muna said.
Queen Acai loved her reply
"We shouldn't have to worry about those three," Muna stated.
"Three?" repeated Queen Acai.
Muna confirmed, "We left Karuk and Azel sprawled on the floor.
They're both bloody as if they went to war."

Pleased with Muna’s account, the Queen said,
“Tell Orion I want him to come see me.”
Muna bowed, then turned around to tell Orion.

Queen Acai looked into the eyes of the people,
She saw devastation and fear.
These were her people.
She dreamed of this ever since she vowed to the Shadows.
As a young girl, there was blood dripping down her head.

“You called for me,” asked Orion.
Queen Acai was startled by what he had asked.
Gaining composure, she leaned over and stared him in the eyes
And asked, “What were you carving in Aiyden’s chest?
Please don't lie!”
Orion stepped forward, fixated his eyes on her, and replied, “Traitor.”
“Why?” She asked
“I saw him talking to Elijah,”
Orion explained, “didn't hear much.
But his mask was off, and I heard him tell Elijah that he was in trouble.

Then Elijah told him he was a follower, not his own man.
I was upset—screamed his name, Aiyden!
Getting a hold of him, I slammed his face against the wall,
Questioning why a homie of mine would cross that line.
Something snapped in my mind,
And I decided I was going to mark him permanently—

<u>Traitor</u>
It started with a line.
No care for his pain
He was no homie of mine
I was going to carve his name
When I cut the T
You should have seen him weep
Followed by R—A—I
In reality, I wanted him to die
Before I could finish
I heard a piercing scream
Dropping me to my knees
I punctured his stomach
Felt it justified
As punishment for a traitor

"We saw Elijah bloody, next to Mrs. Nia, also bleeding,
Blamed him for all the misery,
They sold him into slavery," said Orion.

"I need you to finish what you started and
end his life. Being a traitor crossed every
line," King Ravana commanded,
Speaking for the first time, surprising both
Orion and Queen Acai,
Who loved what her husband just said.
"Yes, I want that boy dead," agreed the
Queen.

He started reminiscing…
"What up, Orion?" asked Aiyden.
"Man, come over to my place, we are
throwing a party tonight.
It's going to be a lingerie masquerade,"
replied Orion.
Daydreaming, he asked himself, *Why did I
even invite my homie to the party?*

"Orion! Did you hear what the King said?"
"I heard him, my Queen," he replied.
King Ravana ordered, "Take care of him.
Once we finish this Poe situation,
I need all your attention."
Nodding in understanding, he left the King
and Queen.

Orion saw the devastation in everyone's face
From the actions that were decided
yesterday.
Judeawai was hurt in the worst way.
The bell's rung, a song has been sung,

"Judeawai recognize your King Ravana and
your Queen Acai."
These words echoed throughout the skies
Mixing in with the moans, groans, and cries.

****

"That was my cousin." The camp heard this
Before the young man got three more hits to
his stomach.
Pouring out of his mouth was vomit.
"My cousin!"
Another clean hit square in his stomach,
more vomit.
Then he turned towards me, yelling,
"Hang that Old Man."
My side was going through so much pain
I started thinking, *I can't go through that
again.*

"Enough!" Everyone looked at the man called Master
"You hit that Old Man, he dies, we lose property, and don't have anything to keep this murderer in check. Let the Old Man rest his wounds from last night. I promise that the slave is going to regret taking one of our lives. His punishment has been brewing in my mind. As I slept throughout the night." said their Master

The man yelling looked at Elijah and said,
“That was my cousin.”
Before hitting him one more time and walking off, he demanded, “Cut him down.”
The Master looked at me and said,
“Nurse this young man back to life.
His life is in your hands.”
Then he told his crew to gather, and he shared his plans with them.

He couldn't hear anything that was being said.
This young man's head was resting in his hands.
Gasping for air and thinking to himself,
I should be dead.
In his ear, he could hear him say—

“I Didn't Do Anything”

Holding this young man was hurting
He knew this one didn't do anything
Honestly, he didn't do anything
Yet he was sent to Deathly Shadows
Because of a dream
“Supreme One, I ask on this devastating morning
To lend me strength for this young man.”
Elijah said one last time, “I didn't do anything.”

Rocking this young man

He promised himself
That he would live for this young man.
If Elijah decided to live
He was going to give everything he had
To live and not die.
Those ropes were tight around his wrist

Looking towards the sky
Praying one last time
To give this young man might
His thoughts got interrupted with spit in his face. The man who almost took Elijah's life blurted, “You better pray he dies!”

****

Judeawai chanted, swallowed in grief.
Some people were protesting in the streets
The image of his mother's death
Ravana could still see.
Caused by a ravaging savage beast
“I will not accept you as the King and Queen. I know what you did last night!”
The crowd started listening to the man who was screaming
“I will expose these fakes—Ravana and Acai.”
The bells stopped ringing; the King’s court stopped singing
“Leaders were...”
“Leaders were what,” yelled Queen Acai.

"SOMEONE HELP ME!"
King Ravana saw all the people.
They were standing by watching his Mother being eaten alive.
His thoughts were interrupted when he heard,
"Y'all are no king and queen of mine."

Furious inside because his mother was gone,
He heard his new wife say,
"How dare you challenge my crown?"
King Ravana balled his fist, leaned back into yesterday, then swung to land a blow to the man in his mouth,
And screamed, "Hit me, if I'm no king of yours,
COME ON, HIT ME!"

The man's swing came slowly, making King Ravana appear to swiftly dodge him.
Then the King's next blow
Ended up breaking his jaw, knocking him to the ground.
Then the King stood over him and knocked a few teeth out.
The townsfolk didn't know what to say now.
King Ravana
Grabbed his knife, pushed it into the man's chest, and demanded—

<u>"Say What You Were Going To Say!"</u>
It sounds to me
Like you have a lot on your mind
You will respect my queen
Your queen now
Do you hear me?
Pushing harder into his chest
There, in front of everybody, his body lay
Looking around, King Ravana said,
"This is what happens when you question the crown."
Staring down at the man, he said,
"Say what you were going to say."

"You killed…Ap….i," he stuttered through streams of blood.
Judeawai couldn't believe any of this was real. Why,
Oh where was the peace…where were the sunny times?
In one day, they couldn't believe how many people were killed.
Over the body, King Ravana stood still
So many bodies were deceased
This morning, the sun did not shine

****

"Mycki!" He was trying to stay low, but the voice sounded very familiar.

"Mycki!" came from the direction in which
the person was yelling.
Mycki took a look around, scanning the
crowd, then he saw him standing there
A guide and a sense of wisdom for Nuka—

Mintz

The right hand of Nuka
The left hand of Aponi
Nuka and Mintz protected Aponi, a lady
now
It was Mintz's idea for Aponi to sit at the
table
Their village listened to Mintz

Running towards Mycki with frightened
eyes
Mintz asked,
"Where is the King and our Queen?"
Mycki couldn't answer the question;
still hoping to be dreaming
"Mycki!" he shouted sternly in his face
A few people started to look in their
direction
"Be quiet," said Mycki, and continued to
say, "Our King Jodi was murdered."
"By whom?" asked Mintz

Agonizing, Mycki began to explain,
"It was nature,
Our lands had caused destruction,

The fire from the skies took him."
Mintz couldn't believe what he was hearing.
"The Queen saw everything. I wasn't there when it happened.
I was protecting our future king."
"From what?"
"Ravana was trying to kill the boy,
So I interfered and saved him.
Ravana did a number on that young man."
"Our Queen?"
"She's safe laying low in a place."
Mintz explained, "We docked last night. When we pulled in, the crew saw smoke, heard choked-up cries, claiming fire fell from the skies."
Mycki replied, "Destruction looked Judeawai in the eyes and claimed many lives."
Mintz was lost, wondering what had happened to a generational celebration of peaceful times.
"Nuka sent a few to find out what was going on."
Mycki thought about what Mintz just said about them docking.
Looking at Mintz, he asked, "Can we get on your ship, escape from this place so we can be safe?"
Mintz said, "We have a safe spot where Nuka and Aponi dwell. This morning, Nuka

took the ship up the coast. He will come back, and then we can get out of this place."

In the distance, they heard ceremonial bells ringing.
"Mintz!" A couple of men yelled as they ran towards them, not noticing Mycki.
All of them had tears in their eyes, saying, "They killed her. Lady Aponi has died."
Mintz stood still. All he could hear was that she got killed, then he asked, "Who did it?"
"It was night when we made it to the temple. We were trying to find the King or Queen, really anybody who could give us any answers. Then we saw twins and a young man dragging out bodies. Actually, it was two bodies, and I couldn't see who they were. The third body I recognized was our Lady Aponi. They dragged them outside and then lit a fire. We had to watch them burn."
Mintz, who was feeling fire in his insides, bellowed, "Why didn't you attack?"
"There were some Royal Guards around, so we left to get some help. We didn't know what was going on. When we went to the dock, we found out Nuka had left for a few days. We decided to find you with this news."
Mintz didn't move; he had nothing to say. Then Mycki remembered the young man who was standing by.

Queen Acai

Your Queen Kathleen is not here.
Mycki couldn't believe his ears.
A natural disaster took our poor King Jodi's life
He heard a woman crying, praying to wake up
The bells kept ringing, they kept singing
King Ravana and Queen Acai
This song was a lie
Judeawai would never accept Queen Acai

One of the men had his mouth wide open. His eyes were focused on the twins standing next to the queen and king.
He pointed and said,
"That's one of the girls who was dragging Lady Aponi."
Mycki and Mintz looked where he was pointing.
That was the twin, who was with Queen Kathleen, who disappeared with Acai
Thinking quickly, Mycki said, "Mintz, we need to hide. If they find the Queen and our future king, both will die.
If their hands do it, there'll be nothing we can do. That's the law."
Mintz saw the smiles on their faces—

They Will Pay

Cursed they will be
Starting today
To the angels above me
This I pray
Bring them misery
They will be punished for those who have been slain
Avenged, you will be Aponi
Hear me from y'all grave
Cursed they will be, they will pay.

Seeing them, Mycki didn't understand
Was all this Acai's plan
Destruction was caused
Generations of peace were interrupted
Mycki heard the man say, "I can't take this."

The bells rung
Some people sung
King Ravana and Queen Acai
This song was heard throughout the skies
The man said, "I will not tolerate these lies."
Walking through the crowd, screaming.
"I will not accept you as the king and queen.
I know what you did last night."
Mintz wanted to tell him to be quiet.
It was too late, and the crowd started listening.
You could hear the murmuring amongst the townsfolk.

“I will expose Ravana and Acai.”
The bells stopped ringing, and the king's court stopped singing
“Leaders were….”
With a loud voice, Queen Acai screamed,
“Leaders were what?”
“Y’all are no king and queen of mine.”
Acai’s voice thundered, “How dare you challenge the crown!”

Before anyone could react, they saw the man get busted lips
Ravana said, “Hit me if I'm no king of yours, COME ON! HIT ME!”
Everyone saw him swing slowly.
Ravana dodged the swing, cracking him in the jaw
Knocking him to the ground,
He kicked out his teeth and stood over him.
The townsfolk didn't know what to do.
Some thought to themselves,
This is a different king.

Ravana grabbed his knife and pushed it through the man's chest
Mycki and Mintz stood there helplessly.
They heard King Ravana say,
“You will respect my Queen.
Your queen now! Do you hear me?”
Then he also said, “This is what happens
When you question the crown.”

Looking down at the man,
King Ravana mocked, “Say what you were going to say.”

From his bloodied mouth, the man struggled to say, “You killed...Ap....i,”
Then King Ravana pushed harder,
More blood trickled from his mouth like water flowing.
All this couldn’t be real; sunny times were gone.
In one day, countless people were killed.
Mintz looked at Mycki when he said—

<u>“Take Our Future and Be Safe”</u>
Lead our Queen to a safer place
Take them where nobody knows them
They need to rest
I will warn Nuka and meet him at the ship
As you wait, your duty will be to take our future and be safe

Mycki headed to where Queen Acai and the rest were staying
To inform her of this news.
Mintz tearfully watched Mycki leave.
It had to be him to tell Nuka his sister had died.
The new Queen and King took the lives of some of the leaders,

And Mintz promised himself they would answer for their crimes.

18. The Escape

Queen Acai peered into the King's eyes,
moved in closer, whispering,
"I'm starting to question your power as king.
It's been a week already, and there's no
Kathleen or Poe.
Where's your revenge against Mycki?
Didn't he beat you in a challenge?"

King Ravana couldn't believe what he was
hearing.
His new wife, how could she say this?
Her words deeply pierced him.
"I've turned this whole town upside down,"
King Ravana whined.
The Queen sighed and criticized,
"Not this whole town;
I need them dead so we can permanently
keep the crown."

Her fingers played over his body.
She was a stunning beauty, laying naked in
their new bed.
King Ravana was aroused.
His anger, he couldn't fight.
"I have all my men looking around.
It's been a week since Jodi died.
Fire falling from the skies,
Killing someone who was like a brother to
me, a couple of leaders were murdered

Also your plan killed my mother."

Yelling back, Queen Acai clapped back,
"That wasn't my intention!"
Running through their door was a messenger.
He stopped abruptly when he saw Queen Acai's naked body.
King Ravana roared, "What do you want?!"
Trying to remain focused, the messenger replied, "We found the creature you described that killed your mother."
King Ravana's mind started racing.
Queen Acai raised up, "Where?"
"Nuka's hideout." The messenger answered.

King Ravana told the messenger to get Orion right away.
As the messenger was leaving, he peeked again at his Queen
Before leaving to do what the King commanded of him.
Stroking her hair, Queen Acai gave him a flirtatious smile
Knowing the messenger thought she didn't see him look at her.
Then she heard someone say, "Queen Acai! I will take your life."
She looked around her room as if she were a madwoman.

Her new husband didn't notice as he was deep in thought.
King Ravana was thinking of the clawing, the eating, the ravaging,
He could hardly believe—

<u>He Had To Watch His Mother Die</u>

Azel and I ran past her
He'll never forget how the monster knocked her over
A last time to call to his mother
When King Ravana saw the clawing and eating
Ashamed they both ran
He tried to return
Yet he was held back by another man
They will say the King's not the same because
He had to watch his mother die

Queen Acai was dressing, yet still ranting,
"What are you going to do since you have the location?"
King Ravana was still thinking
Daydreaming of his mother bleeding.
You've failed your challenge
Now his thoughts were interrupted
By someone at their door.

"King, you needed me?" asked Orion
"I need you to get everybody ready.

I found where that punk and beast have been hiding."
"Yes, sir."
"One more thing, Orion," the King added,
"Yes, sir?"
"We will take care of this first,
Then I need you to take care of your homie when we return.
Do you understand?"
"Yes, sir."

****

"Who stabbed you?" the crowd asked.
There was a lot of fear in Elijah's eyes as they were pointing at him.
He felt a searing pain in his stomach.
Deciding to save his life.
Looking at the scar, he saw the word 'trai'
'Traitor' is what Orion was trying to write.
Still wondering why he had to go out that night.
Going to that party changed his life.

Looking around, Aiyden realized he was in a cell.
After the stabbing, he couldn't remember anything.
How many days has he been sleeping?
He heard footsteps approaching.
"Water."

The footsteps stopped, and one man asked,
"What did you say?"
In a little stronger tone, Aiyden said,
"Water."

The footsteps walked away.
Aiyden was terrified…
Did the man hear me?
But then, he heard footsteps coming back.
The bottom of his door opened.
He saw a cup, when he looked in,
It was spit, and other things were in his water.
Then he heard,
"We don't take demands from a 'traitor.'
Aiyden dropped to his knees when he heard, 'traitor.'
Thoughts zoomed to the lady whose presence made his bones chill.
It was cold in his cell as he realized his life was about to be in hell.
How long have they had me in here,
he wondered.
Leaving his parents to go to the masquerade,
Being anxious when he was supposed to celebrate,
Telling an associate about secret events,
Caused him to land in this place—a hellhole.

He could still hear his mom say,
"Aiyden, maybe you should stay in tonight."

At the time, all Aiyden was thinking about was
Who was he getting into that night?
His ears started to ring when he remembered—
That undeniable scream.
Lying on the floor, his tears began to puddle,
Will they take my life? He wondered.

"Ah! So he is alive."
Quickly, Aiyden looked at the door and saw someone.
They were wearing the same mask Aiyden wore when he warned Elijah.
"The traitor lives," the person scoffed.
Aiyden uttered no words.
"It would've been better for you if you died,
You're pathetic, look at the way you cry."
he taunted,
Aiyden was trying to figure out who was behind the mask.
He thought *it could be Orion*.
"You might have a chance to stay alive."
"I don't understand," Aiyden replied,
"I want you to be—"

<u>My Eyes</u>
For you to survive
I need you to be my eyes
You will be where I can't see
On the outside

Live freely
Your only purpose is to be my eyes

They were waiting for Aiyden's response,
"You don't have that long to decide, die or keep your life."
In this cell, Aiyden knew his life was on the line.
"You're running out of time."
Aiyden declared, "I want my life!"

A door opened and somebody entered.
The masked person hid in the shadows.
Aiyden heard footsteps approaching.
He called out, "Guard!"
"Shut up, you traitor, you're beneath the ground I walk on."
Aiyden stood up and exploded,
"You're a pig! You eat nastier things than what's on the ground I walk on."
The guard ran toward him, hollering,
"You piece of shit!
What did you just say to me?"

At the cell door, Aiyden saw the man's face.
The guard was so angry that he pulled out his knife.
Aiyden flinched at seeing the guard's face pressed on the bars
He heard jiggling keys, then a turn of the latch.

His cell door had been opened, and then he heard, “You don't have much time, go outside and be my eyes.”
He waited a second, then realized everything was quiet,
The hallways seemed empty,
He kept wondering, *Who is helping me?*
Why wear that mask, the one he got from his dad?

Aiyden waited a minute longer before leaving
Hoping nobody was around the corner.
He stayed near the shadows.
Swearing he could feel an evil presence.
He looked around, and saw no one.
Staring down the halls, he ducked down to hide
Every time he heard guards coming.
Finally, he heard,
“The king wants everybody.”
He stayed quiet for a while, knowing capture meant
His lifeless body would be on display.

His heart was racing as he walked up the stairs.
Never had Aiyden been so scared.
Nor did he ever think he’d be an enemy to The Society.
His stomach started hurting,

Twisting and turning at the worst time.
He clenched it hard,
As pain moved throughout his entire body.
Aiyden realized he hadn't moved in a while,
He knew he needed to find a way out.

Another command came,
"I want everybody ready!"
Now Aiyden's heart beat rapidly
So loud that he heard it.
People were talking; steps grew louder as they approached.
Behind Aiyden was the front door.
He opened it and saw the people walking, faces ruined.
In the air was the scent of a shift in the atmosphere.
This was not his Judeawai.

Aiyden grew up in a better place.
It was lively, silly, and witty.
Now, there's defeat in their eyes,
And it's so surreally gritty.
Nothing Aiyden saw was pretty.
He wondered
If his savior was inside,
Wondering,
How could they try to contact him 'their' eyes'?
Then it hit him, and he smiled.
Aiyden was glad to be alive.

Once again, he heard,
"Your purpose is to be my eyes."
The voice was clear; it sounded near.
Yet, looking around and not seeing anybody,
Aiyden felt a sense of fear.
Maybe he should try to find his parents.
Then he thought to himself,
Whoever it was, saved my life,
So I might as well hide and wait for a
message.
In the shadows, he was ashamed.
The fear in Elijah's eyes remained.
He pointed to a man—

<u>Who Had No Blame</u>

Orion told him to point at Elijah
A man who had no blame
For the cut that had him leaking
Devastated by seeing Poe's mother bleeding
The vision of her face played back as he
heard,
"Mrs. Nia!"
Crying to himself, asking,
What has he done?
To a man who had no blame

For any of his pain
Will the heavens ever forgive his wrongs?
He asked the angels to send him to a place
Where nobody could find him,

Not even his enemies or people behind a mask
Trying to be intimidating.

****

“That creature is mine,” King Ravana snarled.
“Get the creature later. First, we kill Poe.
I'll take care of Kathleen; you take care of Mycki,
This is your second chance at a failed challenge.” King Ravana heard his Queen
“Then…torture the creature that took your mother,” added Queen Acai.
King Ravana stormed from the room
He commanded, “I want everybody ready.”

Before Queen Acai left, she walked to where her crown was.
She marveled at how it was made just for her.
A unique crown for the Queen representing The Shadows.
She reached for the crown.
Behind her Queen Acai thought she heard a sound; she looked around,
Nothing was there.
Again, she reached for her crown.
What she heard was a little clearer now—

Fulfill Our Vow

We are the reason you wear that crown
Blood is what we need now
As Queen of The Shadows, make us proud
You've embraced our values
Now, honor your challenge
This is our time, Queen Acai, fulfill our vow!

Hesitating before placing the precious crown upon her head,
She reflected on The Shadow's message,
"This is our time."
She rose and decided to stand by her new King's side.
It was time for Poe to die.

Now she was ready to look Kathleen in her eyes
Before she takes her life.
Years of planning
Now listening to King Ravana yelling
"No life will be spared!"
Vengeance is something they both shared.
It was her turn to ensure this challenge finally got handled.

The twins came to her aid and said,
"We heard we're needed."
"Yes, Queen Acai replied, We found the location of the boy."

Luna was excited by the news.
Since the day fire fell from the skies,
She got to witness so many people die.
Finally, destruction was seen.
Muna asked, “Where has he been hiding?”
“He’s been at Lady Aponi’s brother's location.”
They left following Queen Acai,
Hoping this was the day Poe would finally die.

****

“What was my great-grandmother like?” Aminah asked her father.

My Grandmother

She was a strong woman
A beautiful wife
Wise beyond her years.
Angelic and mystic
She was always there
A seamstress when clothes were torn
The dress she wore was one of her own
On her special day
She loved in such a special way
Always knowing what to do
Smiling like you
Everyone loved my grandmother

Aminah sighed, “I wish I had met her.”

Her father replied,
"You can, she lives in you.
Speak to her and find the reflection for yourself and see the type of woman you will become."
Aminah looked at her reflection in the river.
It wasn't the same as when she would stare
In her great-grandmother's mirror.
"Father, on the morning of my special day,
I recited the forgotten prayer.
The next thing I remember,
I'm flying through the air."

It's been seven days that Aminah has spent time with her father.
She was also worried about her mother,
Whom she hadn't seen since the celebration.
Unable to suppress her anxiety,
she spoke out loud,
"I hope the heavens didn't take her."
"Who are you talking about?"
her father inquired.
"I'm talking about my mother;
I haven't seen her since the celebration."
Looking in the skies, he replied,
"Your mother is a strong woman.
I do not believe those flames claimed her life. I know she's out there searching for her special light,
Baby, you saved your mother's life."
Aminah turned to her father as he continued,

“If you learn to talk to her, your great-grandmother
Can teach you a lot about our history.”

It troubled his heart to see his daughter as she was,
Depressed, sitting in her favorite, now torn, dress.
He tried to imagine how to make it better for Aminah.

Then, he saw a shining bright light and heard a voice
It sounded familiar and had been years since he listened.
Everything seemed frozen in time,
The night his grandmother died played in his mind.

“I’m very proud of the grandson you’ve become
Be a nicer husband, a better father,
You have a second chance with your newborn daughter.
She's irresistible and a treasure.
Would be a lotus
My little me
Let her be free
Listen to your wife—”

Remember This

"Never forget you come from me
Be strong—right your wrongs
Love your daughter; she deserves the world
Honor your family
Stand on what you believe
Never forget the power of prayer
Your ancestors will beckon at your call
I've never told you this:
Love yourself My grandson, remember this.

The light disappeared just as it appeared.
Tears pooled in his eyes and then emptied onto his cheeks.
Aminah realized her father was crying,
So she stood behind him and wrapped him securely in her arms.
Never wanting her father to go through any harm,
She softly asked, "Dad, what's wrong?"
"I just heard something that I've needed to hear for some years."
He thought to himself,
I'm strong and come from my grandmother
Whose blood also flows through my veins.

Aminah hugged her father a little bit tighter.
Earlier in the week it was reported that Judeawai has a new queen
Finding out it was her long lost sister, whom she would never forgive

All thought Acai had died, they found out
Judeawai's destruction they were behind
Her sister's actions hurt her father —

<u>Sir Takoda</u>

To a band of men, he was their leader
A father to two daughters
Husband to a beautiful wife
He stood against The Society
He always wanted the betterment of his community
For some, he was an exceptional teacher—
Sir Takoda.

"There's news of a creature from hell at Nuka's hideout.
We believe the next in line is hiding there."
Flames glowed in Aminah's eyes.
Sir Takoda had no time to say a thing
His daughter replied, "Get everyone ready,
We're leaving now to march to those grounds."
The messenger said, "Sir Takoda."
Aminah looked at the messenger cowering before her,
"You do as I say, get everyone ready;
There are some people I'm prepared to slay."
He ran to deliver the message to the band of men waiting.
Aminah murmured to herself,
Someone is going to answer

For altering who she is now and ruining her special day."

****

"I will torture that creature with my bare hands for my mother,"
King Ravana roared, pulling his sword and pointing it to the skies.
The army was close to the hideout.
Queen Acai knew there was no escape for them.
She imagined her hands around Kathleen's throat,
Desperately trying to strangle her,
While watching as her face turned purple,
Feeling life, leave her body.
Her chance was close.
"Muna and Luna," summoned Queen Acai.
"Yes, Queen," answering in unison, they came running as a pair.
"Run ahead of us and try to find a weak point for entry."
"Yes, Queen," both quickly ran along while appeasing the Queen with a—

<u>Favorite Song</u>
Queen Acai
Will make them die
Before our very eyes
By no surprise

Won't spare a life
We took their light
The dark has come
Her reign begun
We skip around and sing these words
This is her favorite song

Queen Acai began repeating the words.
"Queen Acai will make them die."
"Sir, up ahead we see the creature!"
King Ravana grabbed his bow.
The army started running now.
Queen Acai noticed the King preparing his weapon
He had a specific look in his eyes.
She yelled, "Wait for my signal!"

King Ravana didn't listen.
He grabbed an arrow, pulled it back, and let it go.
He heard his wife scream, "No!"
As it soared in the air, he grabbed another and let it go too.
The first one went through the window.
The second arrow went through the wing of the Sheagle.

King Ravana heard it squealing, lifting itself with its wings.
He was preparing another shot when he heard, "Stop!"

The King didn't realize how close to the house they had gotten.
Jumping off the horse his anger made him run faster, as his only thought was
Leashing consequences for his mother's death.
He was ready for this battle.

The search was finally over.
King Ravana started banging on the door,
After waiting a little while.
He burst through the door with vengeance in his eyes.
Nuka started running full speed towards Queen Acai,
Running through King Ravana's sword, piercing his spleen.
Nuka dropped to his knees as blood poured from his mouth.
Holding his chin, Queen Acai yelled,
"Tell Aponi and Karuk I said hello!"
Nuka fell face down on the floor.

There was more blood to shed.
As Queen Acai walked through the house,
Noises were heard upstairs, prompting her to
Search for heads to cut off.
She felt the blood on her hands.
"We've got to go!" Queen Acai heard Kathleen scream.
"Acai!"

All heard the skies cry.
Right before Acai's very eyes,
She was now standing in her sister's destroyed room.
Everything was knocked over.

Seeing her grandmother's mirror lying on the floor
Enraged Queen Acai stomped the glass out and wept.
Then she shoved the remaining family pictures off the shelf.
Gazing at the destroyed mirror,
she cried out to the skies,
"This was supposed to be mine!"

A figure started to appear, but Queen Acai had no fear.
Then she saw her little sister, but Aminah was not terrified of her.
This girl was ready to fight.
"Acai, come outside!"
Hearing the heavens call her by name caught her off guard.
She had never seen her younger sister stand up for herself.
She had always run to their mother.

"My Queen!"
Yelled a man, who was not her father.
"Acai!"

In front of her was King Ravana.
There was fear in his eyes as he looked at her, “The heavens called you outside!”
Looking around, Queen Acai’s vision was becoming clearer.

She was back at Nuka’s hiding place.
There was no place for Poe and Queen Kathleen to escape
“Poe and Kathleen, you're mine!”
“Acai, show your face!”
Queen Acai ran outside; looking up, she saw Aminah in the sky.
Someone shot an arrow towards Aminah, and her wing deflected it.
Queen Acai could have sworn she heard one of the twins cry.
Aminah looked down at her sister, saying—

I See No Queen In My Eyes
I see a scared older sister
You can no longer bully
Your jealousy altered my being
“Look at me!”
I see a scared coward hiding in the shadows
Pretending you died
After today, they will be unwilling to follow
She flew down and hit Acai with her right
Getting knocked back.
Her older sister realized
It wasn’t all her might

Aminah was prepared to fight
She said I see no Queen in my eyes

Hearing these words caught Queen Acai by surprise.
Her little sister was going to die.
She was going to take Aminah’s life with her knife.
The audacity to strike with the right.
How dare she touch a queen's face?
Queen Acai started to run towards Aminah
With that one wing, she moved faster
Grabbing her and attacking her older sister.
Everyone was watching Aminah.

Queen Acai couldn’t believe it,
She had to find a way to stab her sister.
Aminah knocked her big sister to the ground
And Queen Acai thought,
No one will take her crown,
Especially her little sister.
Aminah moved towards her.
Queen Acai felt the movement.
There was only one way to do it.

She caught her little sister by the wing,
Stabbing her in the arm.
Aminah grabbed Acai by her hand,
Creating a flame.
Burning Acai, her scream was loud.

Then everyone heard a firm commanding voice say—

<u>Ya'll Cut This Out</u>

There's no reason for you sisters to be
tussling around
Aminah yelled, "She took my crown!"
Queen Acai screamed back, "I'm the oldest,
it was mine first"
Aminah said, "She's the reason I'm
disfigured now."
From both her daughters, she could hear
their hurt
Royal blood was fighting in the dirt
Somehow, she had to figure this out
Everyone heard Erykah shout, y'all cut this
out!

Aminah struck Acai one last time.
Erykah knew Aminah wanted to take a life;
She could see the fire in her eyes.
All these years Erykah thought Acai died
There had to be a way to keep her oldest
alive.
As a mother, Erykah knew she just had to
try.
Aminah started yelling, and the ground was
shaking,
And Erykah yelled again,
"I said stop this!"
Aminah heard her mother.

To hurt her older sister was her intention.
She just had to do it.
"Aminah!"
In all her anger, Aminah knew she had to be obedient.
"This can't be fair, nobody will listen," Aminah murmured.
Her mother, who has been there, was always Aminah's—

Reason

If she keeps this up, fire will start falling
Aminah could hear death calling
There was a voice from the shadows
If she keeps this up, more dead bodies will be dropping
Aminah could hear Erykah yelling and shouting
Her great-grandmother's voice came from love
If she keeps this up
Destruction is what she'll continue leaving
Finally coming to reason

Aminah started to calm down.
Queen Acai knew this was the time.
Her anger ignited a fire inside.
For those actions, someone had to die.
When she finally recognized that her father was standing by Aminah's side,

Queen Acai looked at her mother,
And asked, "Whose life?"
Erykah didn't understand what her daughter was asking.
What did she mean?

"Your special daughter struck the queen;
Someone will have to answer for these crimes,
Aminah or your husband.
Whose life will you save?"
Erykah finally noticed the men who came with Aminah.
Then she saw his face—her husband.
She remembered when he left.

"A crime has been committed, the one you choose
Will suffer," said Queen Acai.
Before Erykah could answer, Sir Takoda stepped up
And said, "Take your father."
He was right there, and she could finally hold him again.
Queen Acai smiled and commanded the Royal Army
To apprehend him.
Erykah couldn't watch her husband leave again.
His lovely touches were something she was missing.

The ground stopped shaking.
Aminah didn't know why her sister had to take him.

Erykah knew everything changed when Aminah was born.
It was like her oldest daughter's heart was torn.
"Acai, that is your father!"
She looked at her mother sternly,
"For this strike and that burn,
Someone will be offered."
Two army men grabbed Sir Takoda.
He looked at his youngest daughter and said,
"Remember what I taught you, Aminah."
The men started to pull her dad,
Watching this was making Aminah mad.
How they handled her husband made Erykah sad.
Sir Takoda yelled, "Remember!"
Aminah remembered—

Some Things She Was Taught

Her bloodline is royal
She was born special
Together, they only had a week
Aminah listened every time her dad spoke
In his eyes, she was still his little lotus
With her great-grandmother
She could overcome anything complicated
Learn from those unhealed scars

This was her father
Everyone could feel Aminah getting angrier
Reflecting on some things she was taught

Queen Acai told him that he would suffer.
Sir Takoda saw his wife cry.
It had been years since he was with his wife.
Erykah had always been his world.
They both messed up with their older daughter.
He has to stand on his own, no matter how bad it is.

All this had to be a dream.
Before Sir Takoda left,
He saw Aminah and Erykah together.
He heard his wife scream

****

"Acai!" They all heard the heavens scream.
He heard the voice of his love.
Poe wondered
Why does she sound so far above?
Mintz yelled, "Follow me."
As he led them the back way.
There was so much pain.
"Did Aminah find out what I did that night?"
On his face, he felt the hands of the lady in lingerie.

He heard his lady say, “Acai, come outside!”
Mintz yelled, “This way!”
Poe started praying—

<u>Please Help Us Escape</u>

Father sitting on high
Send angels to keep us safe
To be good, I will try
Forgive me for my mistakes
Today, I do not want to die;
Please help us escape

Acai cried, “Poe and Kathleen,
You are mine!”
Aminah was angry, “Acai, show your face!”
Mintz looked back and said,
“We have to stay alive.”
They opened the back door and began running out,
When the twins blocked their way.
The intentions to kill were in their eyes.
Before anybody moved, they all saw an arrow
Tear through one of the twins' sides.
Poe saw Muna drop to her knees
And let out a horrible cry.
Without a thought, the group ran by,
Leaving her with her sister before she died.

Looking up, he saw Aminah in the sky.

A wing had grown out of her left side.
He heard her say,
“I see no queen in my eyes.”
Poe was wondering why she was in the skies.
“You can no longer bully.”
Poe was confused as to what she was.
Then he heard her scream, “Look at me!”
After a few words, he saw her take a dive.
They finally got away.

He was happy they were alive.
Mintz said,
“I’m going to take y’all to the ship.”
Poe realized he was the reason for this.
He remembered hearing in his dream,
“This is because of your lies.”
His dream was true, including fire falling from the skies.

Why did his mother have to suffer for his crimes?
Poe knew he failed to honor love.
His consequences were flying in the skies.
Was he the reason their king died?
All of them were hoping to survive,
While running faster towards the ocean.

They started tripping when the ground began to shake.

Queen Kathleen remembered her husband being stuck,
When the ground started shaking.
She yelled, "The fire is going to start falling."
Death was calling.

Poe remembered hearing Aminah scream,
"Poe!!! The city will know of your lies."
Then the ground started shaking,
That's when he ran into the man who tried to take his life.
Remembering the last time he heard his mother cry
Before he fell into darkness.

Queen Kathleen started remembering
What the skies had said before her husband died.
"Poe! This is because of your crimes."
Now she realized it was Aminah who brought fire from the skies
Claiming many lives.

Queen Kathleen was playing everything in her mind,
And now, she is blaming the future king for his crimes.
The ship looked more beautiful the closer they approached.
He will answer for King Jodi's life,

Queen Kathleen thought.
All of a sudden, the ground stopped shaking.
One of the men on the ship yelled,
“I didn’t think you would make it!”
Mintz yelled to them,
“We have everybody, let's go!”
As they got on the ship, one of the men asked, “Where’s Nuka?”
Mintz looked at the men, then glanced down and said, “He’s not coming, let’s go home.”

19. A Sea's Tale

"Thanks for saving our lives," said Mycki,
Followed by a pat on Mintz's shoulder.
He smiled, but chose not to reply
After having seen his friend, brother, and family get slain.
How would he tell their mother her children had been murdered?
They cut a family line right before Mintz's very eyes.

Mycki could tell this man was lost in thought.
He was glad all of them had escaped.
They had to get away from this so-called new queen and king.
It was the smell of the sea, and getting used to the rocking of waves
He could tell Mintz was in a whole different space.
There was so much hatred in his face.
"Why did things have to go this way?"
Mycki thought.

Some crew members came through the door,
One asked, "Mintz, what would you like us to do?"
Mycki stared at them, then looked at Mintz, still in a daze.
He pondered,

Should he dare speak to these men?
They don't know me, but Mintz is deep in thought.

"Sir!" One of the men yelled.
Mycki asked, "Have you checked the ship to see if anybody slipped by?"
They looked at him, wondering who was he to question them.
Looking closer, they realized this man was the king's right-hand.
"To be honest, we haven't checked this vessel yet."
Mycki said, "I strongly advise you to check this ship for any possible threat."
Without any hesitation, out the door they went.

After they all had gone, Mycki heard Mintz say, "I'm next."
This threw Mycki's thoughts completely out.
He asked, probing for more,
"What do you mean?"
Mintz yelled as though he wanted the world to hear, "I'M NEXT!"
Labored breathing, sweating, gasping,
Mintz tried to catch his breath and avoid death.

Finally, after getting himself together, he stammered,
"Nuka was next to lead, then this so-called king dropped him to his knees."
Once again, Mycki asked,
"What do you mean by your next?"

"Since her children have been slain,
I am next to lead our tribe."
Mintz explained,
"I wasn't prepared for these times."
Mycki gazed at him when he made that statement and thought to himself,
Who really was prepared?
Seven days ago, it affected so many lives.
Now our only responsibility is to keep the future king and rightful
Queen alive.

Then Mycki's thoughts were interrupted by Queen Kathleen's screams,
"Poe! You're the reason the fire in the skies claimed so many lives!"
Mycki started running with Mintz while he asked, "Why is the Queen outside?"

****

(14 Years Ago)
"Congratulations, Kathleen!
As the future queen of Judeawai,

three ladies will follow in your way.
They will listen to anything you have to say.
These ladies are—

The Future Queen's Sisters

For a queen, these are given sisters
They help out when needed
They're loyal to only you
Their sister will be the Queen
Such duties are to protect you from things
Dangerous and deceptive
They will always give honest self-reflection
Andrea, Ella, and, Aphora were now the
future Queen's sisters

Andrea looked at Kathleen and graciously said, "I'm glad you are going to be our new queen."
Kathleen proudly looked over all three of her sisters
Who came with the crown.
Outside, she heard the people in the city singing;
Joy they were bringing.

In her head, the wedding was still playing, and she saw
All the smiling faces looking at her.
This night was truly amazing.
On the dance floor, Jodi swiped her off her feet.

Today, she said 'I do,' to her future king.

Seven years ago, it was announced that Jodi would be king.
She would be Judeawai's new future queen.
When she was a little girl, this was a dream
Kathleen heard someone say—

<u>This Could Be A Good Change</u>
To change history
My husband found a way
A sign he saw from above
Jodi, will be our first non-royal king
Royal blood flows through your veins
Always think for the best of Judeawai
The city will listen to what you have to say
Kathleen, looked at the wife of Denali
When again she said,
"This could be a good change."

This lady was elegant,
Demanding attention,
And always listened
Careful when she spoke, and when she did,
The people heard hope.
Kathleen was honored to hear these words from—

<u>Queen Kassi</u>
She is a mighty queen

Royalty in her blood, married to a king who had royalty in his
Obeying tradition has always been in place
She stood by the King's side when Denali
Choose to give the non-royal an opportunity
Because of their actions, there is a future king named Jodi.
This came by chance by way of a sign and Queen Kassi.

"My Queen," said Kathleen.
Queen Kassi looked at Kathleen and continued,
"Soon, you will be the queen."
In the distance, they all heard Jodi yelling, "Where's my queen?"

(At Present)
"Queen Kathleen!" Ella screamed, shaking her queen from her trance.
Looking around, Queen Kathleen remembered she was on a ship.
They barely escaped Acai.
When she was running, she noticed an angel in the sky.
Now, she understood that it was there for Poe's crimes.

"Queen Kathleen!"
She saw tears in her sister's eyes.

The air was cold, and they were all hurt that Andrea had just died.
They couldn't believe an arrow tore through her.
The Queen had no time to cope, and before she could say anything,
She thought she heard someone outside.

Through her window, she saw Poe wailing,
"I didn't ask for this!"
Then he fell on his knees as if he were praying.
Queen Kathleen started to get dressed.
Ella, her sister, was confused about what was going on.
She was pacing back and forth; they knew something wasn't right.

The Queen heard in her head,
My actions are the reason you're gone!
Then she blurted out,
"He's going to answer for King Jodi's life."
Ella and Aphora didn't understand what the Queen was saying.
Ella asked, "Who's going to answer?"
As Queen Kathleen ran out of the door, she replied, "Poe."

****

Looking into the vastness of the sea,

Darkness was all he could see.
It bothered Poe that he had to leave Judeawai,
In the city, he always felt safe.
Why did he get chosen to be king?
His decision interrupted centuries of peace.
So many lives were taken because of his lies.

"All I want is you."
He saw a bright light
It was Aminah floating in the sky.
She said, "You were mine. Why?
When I was willing to give you everything."
Poe yelled, "I wasn't thinking!"
The waves crashed upon the ship.
"I didn't ask for any of this!"
Poe fell on his knees begging,
"Please forgive me."

The waves seemed to crash harder.
Poe was getting soaked by all the water.
He heard the voice of his mother,
You are my peace on Earth.
"Mom, I just wanted you to be proud.
Now my actions are the reason you're gone."

Poe thought of his homie Elijah;
He was supposed to find her.
When Poe left the house that morning,

He realized he had not told his mother that he loved her.
The winds were laughing;
waves were crashing.
His injuries were hurting, a reminder that his life was almost lost.

He didn't know where they were going.
It was the first time he felt alone since running away from home.
When he looked up, the stars seemed brighter.
So much of him was required, neither was it desired.

(15 Days Ago)
"Poe, come downstairs!"
The way his mom yelled his name had scared him.
After running downstairs, he saw her standing still.
She had an envelope in her hand.
Then she looked at him and said—

<u>You Are Chosen</u>
When you were born, I knew my Poe would be special
You were chosen to be Judeawai's next
From peasant to royalty, you will also give hope

Peace, you must show and be remembered forever
They will see my little Poe
I'm so proud that you are chosen

When she spoke those words, her facial expression changed.
Poe could see the pain and her excitement fade away.
He didn't know what to say.

Nia was worried about the Tribal Society.
Why would they select another non-royal for the seat?
Most of them didn't like their King Jodi.
She hugged her boy, and he felt the warmth and joy.
Poe asked, "What's wrong?"
In her arms, he heard his mother say,
"Stay strong. Always remember you deserve to sit on the throne."
She held him tightly, not wanting to let her baby go.

"To all of Judeawai, you will show…"
his mother declared.
Poe said under his breath,
"I'll be King and Aminah will be my Queen."
The two had been in love for some time.
She's the only girl to bring light to his eyes.

"Please treat that girl right."
His mother said.

(Present)
The winds were violent now, and he heard thunder in the clouds.
Poe yelled, "I will make you proud!"
In the skies, he heard his mother say, "I love you."

"People died because of your lies,"
he heard Aminah cry.
Poe couldn't forget that he saw his love flying in the sky.
"Poe!"
A wing was flopping to one side.
He knew she was hurt inside.
"Poe! You're the reason fire fell from the skies
And claimed so many, many lives!"
Then he heard King Jodi—

<u>You Are Next In Line</u>
You were chosen for this needed time
Learn your lessons and make things right
Protect life!
In this darkness, please shine bright.
Listen, and I'll guide you
I know how it feels not to have royalty in the bloodline
It doesn't mean a thing

Be a great king; show Judeawai why you are
next in line

"Poe, you took my husband's life!"
When Queen Kathleen approached Poe,
she saw Jodi in the light.
His smile gave her a little bit of life,
"Protect our future king.
I miss you, my beautiful queen."
Queen Kathleen dropped to her knees and
screamed, "Why, my Jodi? Adir did not
need to take you from me."
Before fading, she heard him saying—

My Love Is With Thee

Even though I'm no longer of flesh
My love is with thee
I hold you even tighter
Even though you don't feel me
I talk to you in your dreams
Even though you don't hear me
A shield is over you
Even though you can't see
I hold your heart in my hand
Understand this, my love is with thee

Poe looked at Queen Kathleen and said
"I didn't mean to take the life of our king."
Before she could say anything, Mycki ran
outside
With Mintz following behind.

The winds were howling; men and women were yelling
For answers everyone was dreading.

Queen Kathleen looked at Poe and said,
“You have a lot of explaining to do.”
The ship rocked back and forth.
Waves crashed on either side.
Ocean water was everywhere.
Mycki saw that everyone was drenched.
He yelled to them over the winds,
“I feel it’s best if we all go inside.”

The room they were in was dark.
Poe didn’t know where to start;
some faces he had never seen.
It was difficult to explain the events to Queen Kathleen. He told her of the party
and the mask on the ladies' faces.
That night, he had a horrible dream, and they all listened to his story.

A forbidden love was made.
Then he heard a chilling scream.
And terrible cries from way up high
He couldn’t believe it was Aminah who was in the sky.

Before any questions were asked, everyone was surprised.
They saw a young man getting dragged in.

Mintz yelled, “What’s the meaning of this?”
The crewmen stared at Mycki and, pointing to him, they told Mintz,
“That man told us to look through the ship, and we happened to find him.”

The young man was screaming for his life
As the crew members pulled him with force and might.
He yelled, “I'm one of the Tay, Tey brothers.”
There were bewildered looks on many of the faces in the room.
Poe said, “I've heard of you and your brother
Who challenges people with wit and strength.
One brother is supposed to be really strong,
I've heard he hasn't lost.”

Mintz looked at the young man and asked, “Why are you here?”
Terrified, shaking, and gasping for air, the smell of fear covered him.
Mintz cautioned, “I'm only going to ask one more time. Why are you here?”
It was very silent, and the weather was violent.
Everyone was waiting to hear the young man’s answer.
They only heard the waves.

One of the crew members grabbed his sword and said, “I know, we should throw him overboard.”
Then he started to pull him away from everybody.
“Okay! Okay!”
The young man yelled, so they loosened him.

He explained,
“My brother, challenged a group of people
And was killed by Erak.”
Mycki stood and asked him to repeat himself.
“I said, my brother challenged a group of people,
And Erak killed him.”
“Impossible,” Mycki said, “He is dead.”
Poe asked, “Who is —

<u>Erak</u>

A mask covers his face
He basks in joy from taking life away
He finds there's pleasure in pain
Long ago, he used to walk these lands
Killing and roaming free before the peace
Able to control anybody
Promised to be locked in hell for centuries
The dead fear Erak

Mycki encouraged the man to calm down and tell what happened.
The young man took a couple of deep breaths, then responded
"My brother and I were in the next city over.
We felt the ground shaking.
It was my brother's idea to travel to Judeawai.
A couple of days after the shake, we decided to make our way.
We passed a group of men who were eating.
It seemed as if they were waiting.
Between them and us, an argument happened. A challenge was made.
The options were Tay's strength or —

Tey

The younger brother is full of wit
Cunning in a lot of tricks
The sharpest of the two
My older brother was strong,
Anybody he could slay
He is Tay
I'm second; he paved my way
They named me Tey

"They chose strength.
My brother was ready for the challenge.
Up to then, everyone he handled.
When they moved to the side.

That was the first time I saw Erak standing there in his mask.
He didn't talk, just prepared for whatever.
The leader said,
“If we win, your little brother works for us.
You win, then you have an opportunity to have whatever and save a life.
Tay accepted.
That's when the leader said,
“Ahhh, this is to the death,
Only one will survive.”

The men began to circle us;
there was no way out of this situation.
My brother swung a couple of times.
Then Erak roared
As if he’d lost his mind.
He grabbed my brother's face, smashing it on the stone.
The impact made me freeze.
I've never seen someone get hit so hard.
He stomped on his knee; it was the first time I heard Tay ask for a plea.
Erak stomped on his other knee.
My brother couldn't move.
I didn’t know what to do; never had I thought Tay could lose.
My brother looked at me and said, “Run!”

My feet started moving before the rest of the men noticed I wasn't there.

I ran, I didn't stop. Feeling the cool air,
I knew I was close to the shoreline.
In the distance, I could have sworn I heard my big brother cry out
As if it were the last day of his life.
I ran faster. I knew I didn't have much time
Before they started looking for me.

Then I saw this ship, so I snuck and hid between some cargo.
My thought was to sneak out the next day.
Then I heard commotion.
The crew was talking; they had to go to Judeawai. I stayed low,
Knowing there would be an opportunity to get off when they port.
As soon as we pulled in, everyone was on full alert.
At that point, there was no way to get to shore.
The next thing I knew, we were sailing again. Then these men found me."

Mintz considered all that the young man had said.
He was upset because his brother was dead.
Mintz thought to himself,
The queen lost a husband;
He lost people who were extremely close to him…
Walking back and forth, Mintz said,

"With us, he will go."
The crewmen lifted him off the floor.

Everybody looked weary;
Queen Kathleen looked sleepy.
Mintz looked around and said,
"Well, I believe that's enough
Sea tales for one night.
Let's get some sleep.
We'll figure all this out in the morning."
Before leaving the room,
Queen Kathleen told Poe,
"I know there's more to your story."
One by one, some in groups walked to their rooms,
And even Tey got a place to stay.
Mycki, who was staying with Poe, asked,
"How are you feeling?"
It seemed as if Poe didn't know how to answer his simple question.
He was feeling many emotions, especially those about his mother.

Staring at Mycki, Poe asked,
"How did you know my mother died?"
"Acai told us that your mother had been murdered."
Tears poured out of Poe's eyes as he looked to the skies,
He vowed out loud,

“I will seek to the ends of the earth for the reason my mother died.”
In a dark tone, Poe said,
“I will take as many lives as possible.”
Mycki responded,
“Complete your training, and you will be able to take every single life.”

Then Mycki left, heading to their room and leaving Poe alone.
There were no more voices in the sky;
just wind blowing and howling.
Poe decided to go to his room.
He didn't know what to think,
But his mind was blank.
He wished this were just a terrible dream
And slapped himself just to make sure it wasn’t.
His final thought was that many people will pay for that dreadful day.

20. Poe's Chosen Challenge

This was the first time Muna felt alone in a long time.
There were so many songs
She used to sing to her sister.
Her room felt empty, no one to talk to
Why didn't she protect—

Her Little Sister
Twisted little girl
Someone who understood her world
The real respected her
Pain is what she loved to see
She wanted to disrupt peace
From her actions, lives were taken
A society was shaken
Her light came from the moon
Muna was missing her little sister

The scene kept playing in her mind.
In front of them were Poe and Kathleen.
Out of nowhere, an arrow went through Luna's side,
Dropping to her knees, she let out a horrible cry;
The group did nothing, just left Muna there
To watch her sister die.

"Come on, Muna, you have to believe me,

I found somebody who has a plan to disrupt peace.
They need us for a masquerade."
Muna saw the expression on Luna's face
They always had each other's backs.

Why did Luna have to be done like that?
None of this was a part of any of the plans.
Muna could still see the blood on her hands,
Shaking uncontrollably.
Still in disbelief, she was sore in the core.
The only person she could truly trust is now gone.

Emptiness was creeping in.
How could she continue?
She must.
She was older and led her little sister astray.
Forgiveness will not be given;
All will suffer.
Even if she has to walk through Hell.

There was a loud knock at the door.
Wanting to be left alone,
Muna didn't move.
A couple of more knocks followed.
After a while, she shrank more into herself.

The fifth set of knocks was softer and familiar.
"Come in," said Muna.

The door opened for a second,
Then she heard it close.
Soft feet were walking toward her.
Comforting arms wrapped around her body.
She froze.
"I heard what happened to your sister."
Muna cried out, then she said, "Rose!"
A hand softly touched her shoulder.
The room grew a little warmer.

"My sister was not supposed to be a part of this plan."
Muna whispered as she squeezed Rose's hand,
Then she tightened her grip,
"They'll pay for this," Rose declared,
"All of them."
Muna looked at Rose through swollen eyes.
Their decision had caused so many consequences.
One thing after another.
Muna asked, "When will all this cease?"
Rose replied—

<u>This Is Only The Beginning</u>
More lives will be taken
Sorrow will come to all
The pain of the torturer will be felt again
Cries will be heard throughout the land
A new era has just been born;
this is only the beginning

A young beauty will sing the words.
Rose reminisced about a time at the party with Luna.

(At the Party)
"Tell me you're ready to get into some fun," Luna said excitedly to Rose.
Placing the mask upon her face,
Rose responded,
"I'm ready for this. I wonder what Poe will be like?"
Luna answered,
"He's been drinking all night."
Rose danced around saying
"I know he will slip in this passion."
Both of the girls laughed.
Luna said, "The lady in the shadows told me to tell you it's time."
Rose walked out with a smile, thoughts

(Back to Present)
When she heard Muna crying,
"They will answer for these crimes."
To Rose, Luna was the little sister she never had.
The twins and she did everything together.
They looked after each other.
Now Luna is gone.
This felt so wrong.
Rose knew she would have to be strong for Muna.

"How am I supposed to move on?"
asked Muna.
"We're going to do this day by day,"
answered Rose
As she hugged Muna, they heard knocking on the door.

****

"I'm starting to question your power as queen!" yelled King Ravana.
Queen Acai couldn't believe what she was hearing.
"No, he didn't just throw this in my face," she murmured.
"You didn't kill Kathleen; no blood was spilt."
Queen Acai looked at King Ravana,
then said, "Life was taken.
One of Queen Kathleen's ladies died.
Nuka ran through your sword,
Then fell on the floor."
King Ravana continued ranting,
"The fake Queen Kathleen is still alive,
Poe is still breathing, and that creature is still living."

Queen Acai was getting madder.
She didn't know what to think.
"You let your little sister disrespect you as queen," the King teased.

"In this tone, how dare you speak to me!"
Tears fell from the King's eyes, and then he lamented,
"I had to watch my mother die, and the ones involved are still alive,
And you failed a mission."

As she listened to her husband,
Queen Acai swore she heard a whisper,
Her husband yelling in the background
"You talked about me failing, many times!"
In the distance she heard "Disappoint us."
What was it? This voice she was hearing.
Her husband yelled,
"Because of you, I have claimed lives!"

<u>You Disappoint Us</u>
You failed in your challenge
A task we see you can no longer handle
We gave you everything you wanted
Your crown
The Shadows are not proud
You folded as a queen
Our trust, you must earn; you disappoint us

"Answer me!" Queen Acai snapped right back in her room.
King Ravana was standing in front of her, breathing heavily.
She was looking into his eyes when he grabbed her and asked,

"What are we going to do?"
Rage started rising; she started thinking,
Having to fail like this,
In front of her sister and father...
She ran out of the room.
"How dare you run out in the middle of this conversation!"
King Ravana followed her as Queen Acai continued running.

Some soldiers in the hallway noticed the commotion.
One of the soldiers saw how angry King Ravana was.
He told his partner,
"Let's walk the perimeter.
I don't feel like being around here."

Queen Acai went straight to the dungeon to her father's cell.
He said, "I knew you would eventually come here."
Stared at her father sternly, saying,
"Bow to your queen."
"I will do no such thing," he replied
King Ravana approached and yelled,
"Old Man, you will bow to your queen!"
"What happened to you? Asked her father.
"My beautiful Acai
I thought you died.
Now I found you on the wrong side."

Yelling loudly this time,
Queen Acai pointed to the floor,
“Bow to your queen!”
Looking at his daughter, once again, her father said,
“I will not bow to you. You are no queen of mine.”

“Bring me the prisoner.” She told the guard.
He asked, “Which one?”
She screamed at him, “The traitor!”
The guard froze before answering,
“He escaped.”
Everything was silent, and everyone was quiet.
“When,” she asked,
“You’re telling me he escaped?”
“Yesterday.” The guard answered fearfully.

Her father said,
“Give this up, Acai, there is still time.”
Looking at him, she gritted her teeth,
Then said,
“I’ll torture you until you bow to me.”
Her father stared into Acai’s eyes in search of his daughter
Then said, “You would do no such thing?”
But all could see the anger in her face.
She turned, stomped away, and snapped,
“We’ll see.”

Her father was going to feel hell.

Then Queen Acai walked out of the holding cells and headed towards Muna's room. After banging on the door, she heard the summons to enter.
When the Queen opened the door,
She saw Muna lying on the floor.
Rose was consoling her.
Mummering under her breath,
"She's finally up,"

Queen Acai said, "I have a gift for you,"
As she looked at Muna.
"A gift?" Muna asked.
"Yeah, something to help with your pain."
"What is it?"
Queen Acai grimaced the most evil look as she said, "Torture."
Muna and Rose looked at their queen, bewildered.
What did she mean?
The queen started walking out of the room and ordered, "Follow me."

Listening to their queen, they followed behind. As Muna was walking,
She noticed that since the slaying of Luna, she had not left her room.
Soldiers looked upon her.
Rose was right next to her,

Not by blood, but that was now her only sister.
Both knew they had to look after each other as they wondered
What was going on, and why were they walking to the holding cell?
Looking behind, Queen Acai said,
"I hope my present will do you well."
As they were walking into the old, rusted holding cells, they saw a man.
Then Acai told Muna—

<u>This Man You Will Torture</u>

Do what you want to ease your pain
Make him hurt as you do
It will soothe you
Force him to pray for death
There's information I need
Through these actions,
He will give it to thee, this man you will torture

"Strike this man," Queen Acai ordered Muna.
Muna didn't know what to do.
"Strike this man, I said!"
Muna swung at the man, but when she connected, it was a light touch.
Queen Acai's father started to laugh at her; Muna started to cry.

Queen Acai screamed, “Get her out of here!”

Rose escorted Muna back to her room. The Queen’s father was still laughing, saying, “You're no queen of mine.”
As they walked away, she vowed, *On whatever fateful day,*
he will suffer because he laughed in her face.

****

(A Few Days Later)
“As king to be, how do you feel about this new responsibility?”
“I don’t think it’s all the way clicked,
I’m still digesting everything that happened,” Poe answered.
“I heard what happened to your mother,
My condolences,” said Mintz.

All he could hear was his mother screaming, “Poe!”
His thoughts were interrupted
When he heard Mintz ask, “Do you smoke?”
Poe's thoughts wandered to the last time he smoked.
He was with his homie Elijah.

For a second, he could see the townsfolk

Walking by as the hazy smoke rose in the sky.
Then he thought,
How did the Old Man see the future?
Wasn't Elijah supposed to find his mother?
Where is Elijah?

The smell of the herb was in the air.
Poe was now in the present.
He was getting used to the ship rocking.
Mintz stood there, looking worried.
Poe asked Mintz,—

Why Did You Give Mercy?
To someone you don't know
His life was on the line
Why did you show mercy?
When your men were ready
You were protecting
A man you didn't know
Why Did You Give Mercy?"

Ashes fell into the ocean.
On top of the water, birds were floating.
"When that young man was pleading for his life, all I saw was the pain in his eyes.
Everything he was saying,
I knew, was not a lie," responded Mintz.
"Why not spare a life in these crazy times?"
Poe thought,
for my mother, I'm not sparring a soul.

Mintz could tell Poe's mind was going elsewhere.
Gazing out at the sea, there was a familiar breeze.
He sensed they were getting close to home.
Mintz turned to Poe and said,
"I believe things will eventually turn right,
Because you are our chosen king."
Poe didn't know what to think.

Still, Mintz did not know how to tell the Mother of The villagers about her children.
He knew this type of news was heartbreaking.

"I suggest you start preparing yourself,
I can feel we're getting closer to our destination." Mintz advised.
Before leaving, Poe thanked Mintz for the conversation
And the meaningful words he expressed.
Mintz nodded at Poe as he walked away.

Poe had never been so far away from home,
Yet he could still see his Judeawai.
It bothered him that he had to hide in a strange place.
The sun was going to sleep;
The hues of colors in the sky were such a beautiful sight.

Everybody around was busy getting ready;
It seemed as if nobody had time to look at the sky.
Our chosen king— Poe was reflecting on what Mintz had told him.
Fire falling from the skies claimed so many lives;
This was now his life.
Looking towards the heavens, he asks a poignant question—

<u>Can I Make This Right?</u>
Will I be forgiven for those lives?
Am I capable of bringing peace
Through these hellish times?
Will we wake from Khawlam's hold?
I'm asking as a chosen king.
Can a heart be mended?
What price is a life?
Guide me by the light
All I ask is "Can I Make This Right?"

"What's going through your head, young king?"
Poe saw Mycki walking towards him, but didn't reply.
He just continued to stare at the waves.
"I'm here for you if you ever need some guidance.
I was there for King Jodi in all his trials."

Mycki remembered when Jodi received the crown.
In front of the whole city, smiles on many faces, people celebrating,
Chanting the names of their new king and queen.

"What was he like?"
Poe asked, still thinking about Jodi.
Mycki replied, "He was always unsure if he belonged or not.
The first non-royal king never wanted to mess things up."
"It's not fair that Jodi is not here.
He's the one who chose me,
Leaving me in all this disaster.
I was never after the crown."
Poe informed Mycki.

Mycki saw so much worry in this young king's eyes.
"You will also overcome your trials, he assured."
"Land ho!" Crewmen looked overboard as they approached the island.
The skies were getting dark, and lanterns were all they could see.
Out of nowhere, Mintz inquired,
"Why are all my people on the beach?"
It was the way he said it that made it alarming.

Poe heard one of the queen's ladies say,
"It's been years since we've been on this island."
The other lady agreed, then replied,
"All that training."
They both looked at each other and said,
"Andrea was the most skilled of us three.
If any of us had to die,
Why did it have to be her?"

By the time they pulled into the port, it was dark.
The water crashing on the beach was such a soothing sound.
All the people saw the sad faces.
Looking around, a lady walked up to Mintz and asked him—

Where Are My Babies?
My strong son Nuka
My lovely daughter Aponi
Her husband Karuk
All became leaders who sat at the table
Royal blood in all their veins
A new generation is voting for change
Why were her children left behind?
"Mintz," she asked more firmly,
"Where are my babies?"

There was no way Mintz could tell.

Lady Aveena

The one who took him in
When he had no one
The Lady of this island
Teaching young ladies how to be violent
Protectors of the Queen
Respected amongst the women
A wonderful leader
A great mother
The product of her father, Lady Aveena

Mintz broke the news to her,
That her lineage was cut from the table.
All her children were murdered by
The new claimed Queen.

On the island sand, she dropped to her knees.
Tears were pouring out of her eyes,
That's when she noticed Queen Kathleen.
A friend whom she hasn't seen in a while.
Then realized the queen was by herself.
"Where's the king?" Lady Aveena asked.
"The flames from the skies claimed his life,"
Queen Kathleen replied; then, pointing to Poe
She continued, "He is who King Jodi chose before he died."

The news struck even harder when Mintz told her,

He didn't have the bodies of the slaughtered.
How was she supposed to lay them in
peace?
Aveena looked at her new chosen King
And saw more than the eye could see.

They were at sea a while, and Lady Aveena
knew the crew and everyone
Was hungry, so she said,
"Make more food, let's have a feast."
Mintz was still wondering why everybody
was on the beach.
The last thing she said before walking away
with Queen Kathleen was,
"This will be a celebration for the deceased
and our new chosen King."

Poe stood next to the fire; it felt good being
around some heat.
He never spent long periods at sea.
It was something he knew he would never
get used to.
His stomach started hurting when he smelled
the food.

"Welcome to Komodi Island."
Poe looked up
And there was Mycki standing next to him.
"This is the island where they train the
queen's sisters."

Poe said, "I overheard the ladies talking about training."
"This is not one of those places where when you finish training,
You desire to come back," Mycki said

Poe asked Mycki,
"When does my training begin?"
Mintz took his time to answer because he was distracted by everybody moving and doing something.
Tents were being set up, gathering together; this was different.
It wasn't like anything he remembered.

"Word was sent that you survived the fire in the skies.
I'm still waiting for a reply," Mycki said.
Then Poe began reflecting
On what was said to him,
A celebration for the deceased and him.
"Who was that lady with Queen Kathleen?" Poe asked Mycki.
"That is Lady Aveena, the mother of Nuka and Aponi. She is a warrior and a leader;
Her family have been the leaders of this island for generations."

Poe didn't have anything to say; he was lost for words.
So many lives were taken, hearts broken.

Will he be able to heal a nation?
He thought, what is a celebration without his mother and future wife?
This didn't feel right.
Elijah wasn't by his side.
"Let's get ready," Mycki told Poe.

****

The room shook as she spoke to her mother.
"How dare you still defend her?
Every day, my father will suffer."
"Aminah, your father wouldn't want you to kill your sister."
Deep down inside, Aminah knew her mother was right.
"Why did she have to take him away from me? He just came back into my life after all this time."
Erykah asked her daughter,
"How long were you with your father?"
Aminah replied,
"A week and that wasn't enough time."

Erykah knew what her daughter meant.
For her, years came and went without seeing her husband.
He was protecting the royal blood, but many times she missed his love and those hugs, only to see him taken away.
"Your sister, you cannot slay."

This hurt Erykah differently.
Aminah thought all this was wrong and replied, “He did tell me you were strong.”

Erykah wondered why she had to be away from him so long.
In her marriage, this isn’t what she wanted.
“Your dad always had the right words.
He was never the same after his grandmother died.”
“Yeah, he told me she was wise, a beautiful wife, mystic type,
And was always there,” Aminah said.
“That was a very special woman.
I loved her, and I miss her.”
Right when she said that, there was a blinding light and
Erykah heard a voice that said—

<u>“I Miss My Babies”</u>

In my grandson’s eyes, you are his light
Erykah, you have always been a strong wife
A Wonderful mother
It’s okay, you didn’t know how to love your daughter Acai
She came prematurely into your lives
I saw y’all try
It was a blessing having the opportunity to see the second-chance baby
A lotus, who made her parents better

My beautiful granddaughter, please try to hold everything together
Even in the afterlife, I miss my babies

As quick as it came, the blinding light was gone.
Aminah could sense that something was wrong as tears
Slowly moved down Erykah's cheeks.
This was hard for Aminah; she had never seen her mother weak.
How can this be?
What did her mother just see?
It was the same look her father had.
There was so much pain.

Hugging her mother, Aminah said,
"I will make Acai answer for her crimes."
After wiping her mothers tears,
Erykah said, "No!
It was because of Poe's lies that we had to purge in this fire.
Judeawai had to suffer for his crimes.
I heard you tell everyone when you were in the skies."

Aminah hasn't had much time to think about Poe or her friend Rose.
She was so distracted by her older sister.
Who, in the end, hurt her the most.
Her angel eye turned red and—

She Saw
An angel in the skies
Fire falling all around her
The ground was shaking
Soil was breaking
There was a dead rose
Living amongst the souls, she saw

Judeawai's destruction happened
Because of the lies that have been told.
Now her father suffers. "Everyone will
answer who was involved."
Erykah never saw her daughter this mad.
How could she comfort her youngest
daughter
And protect her oldest, too?
She held her so tight.
Then cried to the heavens—

A Prayer For My Daughters
Adir, please hold me close
I need you near
Open the eyes of Acai
Let her feel for those crimes
Protect your angel
She needs you more than ever
Prayer can change the impossible
Only you can fix the problem
Look in my heart and hear a prayer for my
daughters

The skies opened, and Erykah could hear the roaring.
When this happened, she knew the prayer was heard.
In her arms, Aminah was crying.
Rain started falling.
The winds were howling.
This destruction is your seed,
Erykah thought she heard Nia speak,
Impossible since she saw Nia's soul leave her body, caused by her hands.
Erykah was wondering, *How could this be?*

They've been friends for years.
Erykah remembered when Nia came in fear.
"Nia!"
The screaming from Acai, she did hear.
Love they never gave her.
Wiping away her tears, Aminah got herself together.
And assured her mother with so much determination.
When she said—

I Will Save My Father
The man who looked for her
During one of her toughest times
He is a wise soldier
She had only a week
To learn tips on how to be a good leader
Aminah will gather the men

Spoil all her sister's plans
Declaring "I will save my father"

Erykah believed her daughter.
She just wanted to hold Sir Takoda,
And kiss her husband.
Praying this horrible Khawlam will be over.

****

What a celebration!
Women were shaking; men were moving,
drums pounding,
Remembering why we live our lives.
Grateful for the gift to breathe.
A time to grieve.
Fire dances to the rhythm.

The loss of Lady Aveena's children was
evidently,
Missed by the islanders.
Yet still they were smiling.
Food and drink are passed around
This was a surprise to Poe.
Hearing the joyous sounds, the praise,
A traditional dance, asking for a second
chance.
In sync, they moved as more drums were
beating.
Elders started speaking,

"We are here to celebrate the ones who
sleep. In their life they lived.
We are also blessed to have our king to be."

The people chanted with a loud cry.
That's when they heard roaring in the skies.
Poe thought, *Will the fire fall from high?*

Water was dropping from the rain, and there
was relief.
Everybody was running to their tents,
Soaked from head to toe.
Poe's celebration came and went.
It was cold without his family and friends.

Outside, everyone could hear the strong
winds.
The waves crash on the beach violently.
Questioning if they would be washed away.
Lady Aveena assured all would be safe.
Mintz yelled, "What are we doing on the
beach, and why are we not in our homes?"
Nobody said a word.
Lady Aveena looked at Mintz and said,—

The Demon From Underneath
He makes dreams a reality
With armored skin
Our regular weapons will not pierce
Poisonous teeth are used on its prey when
they're asleep

Delusion is all you'll see
A week ago when the ground shook
This monster awakened
We've heard the cries of the victims at night
There was no way to fight
Running us out of our homes
Making us find shelter on the beach
We are fearful of the demon from
underneath

"We were waiting for help,
Then we saw the ship returning.
Instead of help, I received disturbing news.
I thought a celebration
Could help me forget all this."
Queen Kathleen sat by Aveena.
Queen Kathleen heard Aveena murmur,
"What was she to do for her people?"
The queen thought of her Judeawai and how
she was forced to leave.

In her lifetime, why was there a disruption
of their peace?
Mintz stood still thinking; there was no
solution to the problem.
Poe saw Queen Kathleen brushing the hair
out of her face.
Out of nowhere, they were in the Royal
Room.
Queen Kathleen was looking in the mirror,

Brushing the hair out of her face in the same way.
She asked, "Jodi, what type of king would you like to be?
What do you think will define you?"

An Answer From A Young King
There's a lot against me
I want to be known for my actions as a king
Not just my bloodline
To continue these peaceful times
I will be known for my duty and protection
They will speak on how I love my queen
Queen Kathleen rose from her chair,
Moving closer to Jodi, she said,
"You are a king who is just someone all Judeawai can trust."
The queen smiled ear to ear because
She heard an answer from a young king

Poe, shaken from his vision, sees Queen Kathleen
Still sitting next to Lady Aveena.
He stood up so all could see, then he declared—

"I Will Accept This Given Challenge
My ancestors will help me kill
This demon from underneath
I will show why I'm the chosen king
Adir will help me win

Home will be safe again
That creature won't be breathing
I will accept this given challenge

Poe realized it wasn't him speaking
All looked at the chosen King—even the Queen.
She thought to herself,
There is something special in him.
Lady Aveena responded,
"We are grateful you are here to rid us of that demon."
"I will accompany the young King,"
said Mintz.
He is not ready, Mycki thought.
An image of Poe's lifeless body next to Ravana's feet
Flashed through Mycki's mind.
Also thinking,
He just received a king's healing from our queen.

"Mintz, we cannot allow you to go on this mission. We need you safe, you are next to lead," Lady Aveena affirmed.
Mintz knew she was right; all her children had just died.
And now the seat to the island was in jeopardy.
It wouldn't be wise to go on this journey.
Poe then bowed to his elders and said,

"I will be known for my duty."
Queen Kathleen looked at him, searching for her husband.

"He will need help finding our homes," Mintz suggested.
Aveena agreed with him, then instructed, "Choose three crewmen."
It was decided that three crewmen and Poe would leave in the morning.
Everyone went to sleep, and Poe went to his tent to think about the challenge that was accepted from within.

The storm kept going.
Poe was yelling in his head,
"*Do not control my body again!*"
Jodi responded, "*The crown is now declared yours. I'll teach you what a king fights for. Don't run, conquer. Learn any obstacle. As a future king, it's possible.*"
Then he heard someone ask,
"Can I come in?"
Poe yelled out saying,
"Do not control what comes out of my mouth again!"

It was Tey at the front of his tent, poking his head around the tent
Looking for whom Poe was yelling at; surprisingly, no one was there.

Frustrated at the situation, he asked Tey,
“What are you doing here?”
“I personally wanted to tell you, you’re courageous. That bravery reminded me of my brother. I can’t live with myself knowing I ran away to be a stowaway, and your actions have shown me you will be a mighty king,” said Tey.

Poe reflected on everything Tey had just said and realized
It wasn’t his choice to face a demon from underneath.
He was not ready to be king.
Then he remembered
The question Elijah asked him:
“What type of king will he be?”
Those sins from that night rained fire from the skies and destroyed so many lives.

“Thanks for stopping by.
I've got to be ready in the morning.
That’s when we’re leaving.”
Tey left after giving his respect, leaving Poe to dwell in all his mess.
Instead of living in this stress,
Poe decided to relax in his rest.

****

"Good morning, Queen. I've heard you wanted to see me."
Queen Kathleen resided in a tent for her and the ladies.
"Mycki, I think I'm going crazy.
I believe Jodi is using that young man."
"Using that young man?" replied Mycki.
Queen Kathleen explained,
"That wasn't Poe who stood to volunteer.
I believe Jodi controlled his body,
even in death.
I know my husband.
It was the way he looked at me.
I saw Jodi in him when I gave him the king's healing."

Mycki didn't know what Queen Kathleen was saying.
He wondered, *How could this even be?*
"I wanted to let you know," Mycki confided to the Queen,
"I feel it's best if I accompany Poe on his journey."
Queen Kathleen inquired,
"Well, what about me, I mean, us?"
Mycki looked at her and the ladies,
then said, "You'll be safe.
I want to make sure that Poe will be okay."

She knew he was right; this island makes killers, so why were they so afraid of this demon from underneath?
Queen Kathleen replied, “We’ll be fine.”
They both knew she was right.
Mycki left them after being assured they would be alright.

Mycki felt the cold that morning, walking to Poe’s tent.
He thought about Jodi; none of this was supposed to happen.
They were supposed to spend another seven years together.
The guide to protect the king's life has failed at his job.
Even though nature delivered the strike,
he should’ve been there.
Then Mycki thought to himself,
If I were there,
Who would have protected the next heir?
Although his mind was full, he was grateful for the fresh air.
It just wasn’t fair.
Opening Poe’s tent, he saw—

A Friend Lying There

Eyes opened, it was like he was waiting for him
His smile is a little different
Familiar in a way

He heard what the man had to say
"I will protect this life.
What I need most is for you to protect my wife
Teach him right.
Thank you for saving our next heir"
Mycki was grateful for a friend lying there

Knocking over his shoes woke Poe up by surprise.
It seemed as if he just closed his eyes.
Poe thought, *why am I sitting up?*
"You don't have to prove anything,"
said Mycki.
Getting out of his pallet, Poe replied,
"I accepted the responsibilities of a king."
Waking up prepared for this chosen journey.
Poe was getting ready, then he pushed past Mycki.

Poe found himself standing in front of Lady Aveena, Queen Kathleen, Mintz, and the three men,
One of the armed crewmen introduced himself as—

Luther
A man of honor
He promised to keep Poe alive
Being at sea for a long time
Built up anger inside

I will cut off the demon’s head
Who took our family and friends' lives
Generations will pass by
This village will tell the tale of Luther

Queen Kathleen prayed for them to be safe.
She looked at Poe and said,
“Have no fear when you look danger in the face.”
Then they sent them on their way.
Luther saw how tired Poe was, so he told him,
When they get into town, that would be the time to rest.

****

The fire felt warm, and his wounds were healing from the attack.
He could feel the cold weather.
Someone came to check if he was better.
Trying to sit up with all his effort,
The Old Man sat next to him.
Elijah asked the Old Man,
“When did you start visioning
The fire falling from the skies?”
“Most of my life. It used to make me go out of my mind. Most folk believed what I said was lies, when I first told them about the fire from the skies. There have been visions and dreams, but I could never see the chosen

king."
"I thought you were crazy when I saw you walk by." Elijah replied
"The fire from the skies verified that I was sane."
"I didn't do anything; someone framed me for my crimes."
"Yes, this I know, that's the reason I've decided to help you.
I will give you my aid. All I ask is—

Survive Deathly Shadows

You will have to leave your humanity
I will protect your sanity
Win all of your challenges
Learn to control any situation
Young man, you will not be the same
They will not take your life
Plot your revenge when you survive Deathly Shadows

Tears poured out of Elijah's eyes.
Why did he have to take a life?
This whole situation wasn't right.
"Help me?" he asked.
"I want to teach you everything I know."

A Tale Of An Old Man, Young

My mentors taught me the skills to stay alive
They all loved me until I started to lose my mind

At a royal table, I no longer had a seat
Our King at the time despised that I told him about this fire
Falling from the skies
A chosen king.
People I loved turned on me
After that, I decided to drink, fall into despair, and die.
Elijah listened to a tale of an old man, young

"What have I done?" The young man asked.
"You survived, stayed alive.
Every day, do that,
And we can find a way to get through this."

Elijah still felt the snapping of his neck, the smashing of his face.
Why were the heavens condemning him to this place?
The men in the camp were coming their way.
"Good morning," the Master said.
"We traveled all this way, and I'm still surprised both of you are not dead."

Elijah thought of what the Old Man just said. "Deathly shadows we will make home."
Looking at Elijah, the Master said,
"I'm going to make a lot of money off you."

The men surrounded Elijah and the Old
Man.
"We've decided there's only enough food
for one of you to eat.
So who shall it be?"
Looking at each other, neither knew what to
think
Both have been badly beaten.
Elijah yelled, "Feed the Old Man!"
The Master said, "This is what you don't
understand, that was already our plan.
Now, eat, Old Man."

The Old Man started to eat, but very slowly.
Every time he chewed, everything was
hurting.
One of the men grabbed Elijah by the head,
shoving it in the dirt,
And yelled, "Eat!"
Their Master told the Old Man,
"However long you take to eat,
This slave will be eating dirt."

The Old Man could see the pain in Elijah's
face.
"You better not waste it,"
The Master warned.
"Yeah, eat your breakfast,"
Said the man holding Elijah's head.
The faster he ate, the more his whole body
ached.

Trying to hold himself, but his arms were shaking.
The Old Man was nervous.
“Eat everything!” Yelled the Master.
Amongst the men was laughter
When I’m done, he’s done,
the Old Man thought.
All this was wrong.
When he had finished, they left both of them alone.

The Old Man sat next to Elijah with his bloody dirty face.
“Working together is the only way,”
He said and threw Elijah some bread.
Survival was the only thing Elijah was thinking.

****

(A Dreamy Like Sequence)
“I’m just saying if I were your man,
you would not have been alone the night of our ceremony.” said Elijah
Aminah looked at him and said,
“Stop playing, you know he’s your friend.”
“That he is, and I told him I couldn’t make it to the party tonight.”
Aminah asked, "Why?”
“So you and I could spend some time together,” Elijah replied with a smile.

Then he asked,
"Have you ever considered giving us a try?
Everything will change after tonight.
He will be the cause of the fire from the skies."
Before she could say anything,

(Open Your Eyes)

Everyone was screaming, "Open your eyes!"
Everything was blurry, and as Poe tried to gather himself, he heard,
"Wake up and open your eyes."
The men surrounded him, and Luther was amongst them.
"There's something outside,"
He heard one of the men say.

That moment, something came crashing through the wall at great speed.
One of them got grabbed.
Luther yelled at Poe, "Let's go!"
As quickly as he could,
Poe picked himself off the floor.
Snatching his pole, he ran out the door.
The two men he followed were swallowed by darkness.
How long did I sleep, Poe thought.

Walking to the town turned out to be a distance.

When he saw the town, it was different from
his Judeawai.
No one was there; it was empty.
All who lived in this town were on the
beach.
By the time they settled in an empty home,
Poe was ready to sleep.
Luther told the other two to look around, but
told Poe to rest.
So he rested.

Pitch black was all he could see.
What came crashing through the wall?
Poe wondered.
"Keep up!" He heard Luther order.
The other man asked Luther,
"Where should we go?"

Sir Luther led them into another home.
Crouching down, whispering to everyone to
stay low.
Everyone was breathing heavily,
trying to calm down.
Listening for any unfamiliar sounds outside.

Poe thought maybe they got away.
Surely this had to be a safe place.
It was so uncomfortably quiet.
Poe was tired of all this violence,
So he closed his eyes; then he heard a
female voice.

(A Dreamy Like Sequence)
When his eyes opened, the room changed.
A lady was standing in lingerie,
dancing in front of him.
Looking around, there were no men,
just women talking,
Walking, dancing, and drinking.
Such beautiful shapes, with a mask to cover
their faces.

One of the women said, "Come here."
Everything was so real;
Poe just wanted to feel.
Maybe get temporarily healed.
The lady was still dancing and getting
closer.
A little louder, one of the women said,
"Get over here!"
Music was playing.
What if this were a second chance?

(Get Over Here!)
"Poe!" All he had seen just disappeared.
Someone pushed him to the floor.
At that moment, the creature crashed
through the window.
Its teeth sank into the other man's flesh.
Poe heard Luther shout, "Get out!"
He wondered *why that man sacrificed
himself.*

Poe ran as fast as he could, knowing he had
to reconnect with Luther for survival.
He thought, *Where could he be?*
Then Poe heard Luther say, "Follow me."
Zigzagging, Luther took Poe through a cut
and a couple of corners.
Maybe they were lost.
Luther told Poe this should be a safer place.

Outside was getting a little brighter with the
moonshine.
Poe saw the worry in Luther's face.
Once this man stood tall and great,
Now he's cowering weak,
Mumbling when he speaks.
In an intense whisper, Poe asked him,
"What was that thing?"
Luther answered—

Something I Never Thought I Would See

It was always a myth to me
This island was named after a demon
A vicious killer
Eating everything
Human weapons have no effect
Stories were told through time
That monster poisoned the mind
We were grateful this creature died
Komodi is something I never thought I
would see

"How can this be?" Poe questioned.
Luther responded, "You're next in line; you have to survive."
Outside, Poe heard cries
"Don't listen to the noise
Komodi plays with your mind."
Poe didn't understand
The noise was getting louder
Poe closed his eyes and covered his ears

(A Dreamy Like Sequence)
In front of him, Luther started to burn alive.
The flames engulfed his body.
What was he to do?
This had to be a dream.

A Hellish Khawlam
Please let this be a warning of what's to come
If I have a chance,
I'll change everything that's been done
Peace, I yearn
My lesson has been learnt
Why do I have to watch this man burn?
Wake me from this deadly dream
I'll be prepared for the celebration
Ready to be a king
There have been nothing but regrets since all this began
Take me out of a hellish Khawlam

The house began to burn
Fire trapped Poe inside
Poe looked around
Thinking to himself, *where will he go?*
Luther was reaching for him
Poe felt helpless in this moment
There was nothing he can do
Flames wrapped Poe up
He couldn't move
Will this be his end?

(Wake Up!)
Wiping his eyes
Poe heard Luther yell, "Run!"
Finally focusing on what was around
Komodi, the demon from underneath
Was standing in front of Poe
Luther was being bitten by its teeth.
He tried to yell 'run,' but more blood seeped.
How was he going to help?
Jodi! he yelled to himself.
He grabbed his pole and pointed it at Komodi.
The energy he was feeling, body tingling,
He had to save Luther's life.
It hurt watching Komodi take another bite.
This demon was toying with him
There was a question he heard being asked,
"Are you ready for this fight?"
Hearing Jodi's voice

Poe said,
“Help me with the lightning strike.”
Jodi responded, “Find it within yourself.”
That’s when Poe knew he was alone.
Another bite, Luther tried to fight.
It was a difficult feeling
Knowing he couldn’t save Luther’s life.

Poe was watching this man cry.
Mouthing one last time, “RUN!”
Poe ran fast before the monster focused on
him.
What did Jodi mean from within?
He was all alone.
Trying to find a deserted home to hide in.
Poe didn’t know where to go.
Can this demon smell him?
How did it find them every time?
Going into a home, then leaving for another.
Was anywhere safe?

He just had to try.
Praying for somewhere he could go inside,
Deciding to go inside one off to the side.
Entering, he ran and hid in the corner,
closing his eyes.
In the distance, he heard his mother cry.
Maybe they lied, and she’s still alive.
“Poe, where are you?”
Trying to find any courage inside.
“Poe!

He had to protect her from any danger outside.
He ran out of the home with his metal pole.
Where did she go? He thought.
Komodi will not get his mother.
Rain started to pour.
"I'm over here," and when Poe turned around,
Standing in front of him was Komodi,
The demon from underneath.
Blood was dripping from his teeth.
At this moment, Poe couldn't move.
How could this be?
Komodi was smiling and asking,—

<u>"Are You Ready To Die</u>
Are you prepared to answer for your crimes?
I've judged you
You're responsible for so many lives
I hear your mother from beyond
There's laughter amongst the women
Anger in a king
I'm answering a plea
Sheol has released me; are you ready to die?"

Poe held tighter to the pole.
Wishing he could control the lightning.
This demon was very frightening.
Both heard a squeal from the sky.

The same squeal he heard when he had escaped.
Such a high-pitch sound.
He felt a thud when the creature landed on the ground.
Walking between Poe and Komodi.
The demon from underneath was getting angrier.
In this rain, his body was steaming.
Komodi snapped, nearly missing the creature.
Its wings flapped,
Out of its paws Poe saw razor-sharp claws.
The bird-like looking dog started flying over Komodi.
Using its claws, piercing through its armor,
Hurting the demon.
Poe could hear it screaming.
The creature was still squealing.
With its sharp beak and K-9 teeth,
It started biting the demon.
Rain was still pouring.
Poe struggled to control his breathing.
Why was this creature from above protecting him?
What did Jodi mean by *it's within*?

Komodi winced
When the creature tried to lift him
Dropping it on the floor.
Continuing to do this action a little more.

Poe heard some breaking of bones.
Thanking the heavens that he was not alone.
Komodi was bleeding, there was no fleeing.
Hopefully, the demon was dying.
The creature from above was trying.
This fight started to get more violent,
When Komodi got a hold of the creature's
wing. He heard a higher squealing
Poe knew the creature that came to save him
was hurting.
He heard his mother's voice—

<u>Help Me!</u>
My little boy
Our future king
Please help me
You will always be my little baby
I'll be by your side
If I survive, I will help you fight
Take you to different heights
My Peace On Earth. Help me!

Poe's body started shaking;
He felt a surge of energy.
All over, he was feeling tingling.
The demon finally had the upper hand.
Poe was the only one who could save this
creature's life.
He needed to find his strength inside.
Komodi has claimed too many villagers'
lives.

It killed the three men he was with.
He will skin that metal coat,
Those lives will be avenged.

<u>Poe's Chosen Challenge</u>

He knew this demon was dangerous
Trying to clear any venomous thoughts
Utilizing everything he's been taught
Never run from a challenge
Whatever the obstacle, he can manage
Poe decided to throw rocks at the demon's face
Praying that the creature could escape
If he dies, this will be his fate
Poe's mother always told him
That her son would be great
Komodi was walking towards him
Looking for the power within
Wondering why in this fight
Jodi couldn't join in
The demon started running.
His pole was pointing
Still no lightning.
Komodi was going to eat him
He started thinking of home.
Aminah, Elijah, his fallen king, a hurting queen.
Then this angel came when he thought of his mother's life,
Right before Komodi could strike.
His angel caught the demon by surprise.

Holding it down, this was the only chance
For Poe to produce a lightning strike.
He felt a surge of energy.
Just in time, the angel let that monster go.
Poe and this bird-like dog creature watched
As the demon fried on the floor.
Both were excited that they survived
Poe's chosen challenge.

It was he who took such a demon's life,
Poe reveled at the thought.
He was drenched in rain,
At that moment, he felt so much pain.
Still thinking of Luther and the two men
who were devoured.
That energy—never had he felt so much
power.
Poe decided to break off one of Komodi's
claws, breaking out all its small razor teeth,
He skinned the coat,
Then put on the coat of Komodi.
For Poe,
It was now armor that regular weapons
couldn't penetrate.

The wind was blowing, making it very cold
to his skin.
Thunder echoed through the skies
Grateful to be alive

My Prayer
Adir thank you for helping me survive
With you above I am not alone
I pray for guidance to the throne
Lend me strength
To fix this
I am insignificant
Adir I hope you hear
My Prayer

Rain was still pouring, he was shivering,
His teeth were chattering.
Then he felt something warm beside him;
It was his angel
Who came from the skies,
Ensuring he didn't die.
One wing shielded Poe, and he didn't feel
the water anymore.
Poe knew he was covered—

They Had An Understanding
They will protect each other, and together,
they will ride
With this angel,
He can soar higher in the skies
Defending all with a lightning strike
With one another, Poe can be a mighty king
There was a reason he was chosen
To everyone who decided to disrupt peace,
Poe promises all will answer
Without any communication,

They had an understanding

Author Take On the Story

I wrote The Omitted Tribe Stories because I was inspired by the idea of Dante's Inferno. The concept of hell, mythology and love has intrigued me for a long time.
I still haven't read the book yet for the purpose of not being influenced by his work. For the art of poetry, I enjoy writing my story. These characters have grown with me. This journey of Poe is very interesting to write with his supporting cast.

As a poet I want to leave a footprint in the culture of poetry such as Sir. William Shakesphere, Langston Hughes, Dante's, Edgar Allen Poe and Maya Angelou.
I'm so grateful that I won the Las Vegas Black Music Awards for best male spoken word artist. This was the first year they awarded a male spoken word and female. My goal was to create some works on par with the Odyssey and let my story be told through generations using the language of today. Writing Sheol pt. 2 was really exciting

I also appreciate Royal Media Publishing for being there for me and providing all the tools I need. Thank you to B. Francheska White for editing this work and giving great advice to improve my writing. Once again I want to thank Gad Elite Book Covers for another amazing cover and being there through my journey. I'm thankful for my family, friends and fans who continue to encourage me to be better.
More work to come.

Epilogue

~~Christmas~~

BROOKS CRITTENTON

Christmas

By: Brooks "TLK Poetry" Crittenton

"It is Christmastime
For girls and boys
We make them beautiful toys
Mr. Clause says it brings lots of joy
It is Christmastime
For the families
We provide their needs
And been changing lives for centuries
It is Christmastime
For the girls and boys"

"Stop singing!" All the elves looked at Oakley, the #1 of all the elves, as he knocked beautiful hand-crafted toys off the shelves with a swift sweep of his arm.

"I can no longer slave over these ungrateful children; our purpose is to make toys and bring joy for seconds."

A few elves decided to stop working and listen. An assembly line of elves was the only thing he could see. Oakley decided to break more toys. He knew this Christmas was going to be very different. So many girls and boys were on the naughty list.

“These children don't believe Santa exists!” Banging on the table, he started screaming, "I can't take this, Nick!"

All the elves were shocked. Nobody called the big guy by his first name, well, except his wife.

"Nick!" Bells started jingling, and they heard big feet approaching.

Oakley waited seconds more before yelling again, "N-I-C-K!"

All the elves heard the robust “Ho, Ho, Ho” resonating from Mr. Clause. One elf alerted, "Santa is coming!"

The elves heard more jingling and “ho, ho, ho's” before the big guy stepped through the door. He wore black boots, a long-sleeved red shirt and pants, and a wide black belt with separate shiny gold tinkling bells all around it. His large hands rested on his bulging belly as he surveyed the room. He saw a few elves working, and others stood still, gazing at him. Aware something was wrong, Santa asked Oakley, "What's with all the yelling?"

Oakley responded, "We're not making any Christmas toys this year."

Santa looked at his #1 and laughed, "Ho, ho, ho! What are you talking about? We bring joy to the girls and boys."

Oakley angrily yelled. "But not anymore! There are more kids on the naughty list, and most of the kids don't think you exist."

Santa said assuredly, "They're children who still believe, and they will receive their dreams. Those are my nice kids who listen to their parents. Aren't they deserving of those things?"

Oakley looked at Nick and said, "I speak on behalf of all the elves; we will not make another gift!" Everything stopped. Toys dropped from a few hands of the elves.

Santa slowly bent down and picked up a toy off the floor. "I will not let any of you ruin Christmas for those boys and girls and my love for the men and women." “Looking at all the elves,” he asked, "Will you help me spread the love of Christmas to these deserving people?"

The elves started picking up the toys, getting back in line, making toys, and singing songs. They all said, "Ol' Saint Nick Christmas is still on." Oakley stood there by himself, listening to them continue to sing.

“It is Christmastime
For girls and boys
We make them toys
Mr. Clause says it brings them lots of joy
It is Christmastime
For the families
We provide their needs
Been changing lives for centuries.”

None of the elves had Oakley’s back. So, he spoke on their behalf. Looking at Mr. Clause, he said, "I will go, but I will not forget. I will ruin your Christmas."
Santa told Oakley, "You could never ruin something so magical."

Oakley turned and stomped away and yelled, "And Rudolf is getting old!"
He heard Santa let out a series of resounding ho, ho, ho’s, followed by boisterous laughs from all the elves.

Oakley was mad! Never had he been so angry walking away from the only thing he knew.

More Books by This Author

POETRY'S POESY
PRESENTS
T.R.P SERIES
CITY OF GOLD

Poetry's Poesy
VOLUME 1
SCATTERED THOUGHTS
I AM A Poet
Effects of Love
Monster
Cain
Disconnect
Felicia
Nightmare
BROOKS CRITTENTON

Poetry's Poesy
VOLUME 2
SCATTERED PRAYERS
Real Me
Women of My Village
Broken Commitment
Paean
Devil's Armpit
House of David
Failed
My Family
Coming Vessel
Hagar
Baptism
Deborah
Abba
Mercy
That's All They See
Innocence
COVID-19
Rachel
Goddaughters
Politicians
Myrrh
Homeless
Lost Sheep
Rebekah
Running
Besties
Iniquity
Fasting
Royal Media
Addiction
BROOKS CRITTENTON

Coming Soon!!

www.ingramcontent.com/pod-product-compliance
Lightning Source LLC
LaVergne TN
LVHW020712110826
845149LV00012B/2224

* 9 7 8 1 9 5 5 5 0 1 3 9 2 *